P9-DVD-823

MAY 3 0 2014

WITHDRAWN

JUN 17 2024

DAVID O. McKAY LIBRARY
BYU-IDAHO

PROPERTY OF:
DAVID O. McKAY LIBRARY
BYU-IDAHO
REXBURG ID 83460-0405

At Issue

The American Housing Crisis

Other Books in the At Issue Series:

At Issue

The American Housing Crisis

Louise I. Gerdes, Book Editor

GREENHAVEN PRESS
A part of Gale, Cengage Learning

GALE
CENGAGE Learning

Farmington Hills, Mich • San Francisco • New York • Waterville, Maine
Meriden, Conn • Mason, Ohio • Chicago

Elizabeth Des Chenes, *Director, Content Strategy*
Cynthia Sanner, *Publisher*
Douglas Dentino, Manager, *New Product*

© 2014 Greenhaven Press, a part of Gale, Cengage Learning.

WCN: 01-100-101

Gale and Greenhaven Press are registered trademarks used herein under license.

For more information, contact:
Greenhaven Press
27500 Drake Rd.
Farmington Hills, MI 48331-3535
Or you can visit our Internet site at gale.cengage.com

ALL RIGHTS RESERVED.
No part of this work covered by the copyright herein may be reproduced, transmitted, stored, or used in any form or by any means graphic, electronic, or mechanical, including but not limited to photocopying, recording, scanning, digitizing, taping, Web distribution, information networks, or information storage and retrieval systems, except as permitted under Section 107 or 108 of the 1976 United States Copyright Act, without the prior written permission of the publisher.

For product information and technology assistance, contact us at

Gale Customer Support, 1-800-877-4253
For permission to use material from this text or product, submit all requests online at
www.cengage.com/permissions

Further permissions questions can be e-mailed to permissionrequest@cengage.com

Articles in Greenhaven Press anthologies are often edited for length to meet page requirements. In addition, original titles of these works are changed to clearly present the main thesis and to explicitly indicate the author's opinion. Every effort is made to ensure that Greenhaven Press accurately reflects the original intent of the authors. Every effort has been made to trace the owners of copyrighted material.

Cover image © Images.com/Corbis.

LIBRARY OF CONGRESS CATALOGING-IN-PUBLICATION DATA

The American housing crisis / Louise I. Gerdes, book editor.
    pages cm. -- (At issue)
  Includes bibliographical references and index.
  ISBN 978-0-7377-6818-3 (hardcover) -- ISBN 978-0-7377-6819-0 (pbk.)
  1. Housing--United States--Finance. 2. Mortgage loans--United States. 3. Financial crises--United States. 4. Home ownership--United States. I. Gerdes, Louise I., 1953-
  HD7293.Z9A55 2014
  363.50973--dc23
                                       2013042524

Printed in the United States of America
1 2 3 4 5 6 7 18 17 16 15 14

Contents

Introduction

In the Declaration of Independence, Thomas Jefferson, the document's principal author, wrote, "We hold these truths to be self-evident, that all men are created equal, that they are endowed by their Creator with certain unalienable Rights, that among these are Life, Liberty and the pursuit of Happiness." For many Americans, this declaration is the foundation of the American Dream—the belief that through hard work all American citizens can become prosperous, regardless of social class. For many Americans, owning a home is an important part of that dream. Indeed, some claim that "the desire for a home of one's own is hard-wired into the American psyche."[1] According to history professor Vincent J. Cannato, "In early America, to be a renter was to be dependent on a class of landlords, and so not truly one's own man."[2] Cannato claims that even Jefferson's political adversaries John Adams and Alexander Hamilton believed that the tenant-landlord relationship smacked of feudalism. Indeed, Walt Whitman, American poet and essayist, wrote, "A man is not a whole and complete man unless he owns a house and the ground it stands on."[3]

The desire to own one's own land and home motivated many Americans to settle the western frontier in the 1840s and 1850s. After the Civil War, personal homeownership grew as builders began to construct homes outside of cities in what became known as the suburbs. Technological innovations such as the cable car and the electric trolley also made it possible for people to commute quickly and cheaply to the city. Nevertheless, lending practices of the time made it difficult for many middle-class Americans to own a home. The govern-

---

1. Vincent J. Cannato, "A Home of One's Own," *National Affairs*, Spring 2010. http://www.nationalaffairs.com/publications/detail/a-home-of-ones-own.
2. Ibid.
3. Ibid.

ment prohibited nationally chartered banks from making real estate loans, and most state banks required a 50 percent down payment and short repayment terms that few Americans could afford.

After World War I, however, the government, prompted by leaders of both parties, began to aggressively promote home-ownership. In the years since, analysts have vigorously contested whether the promotion of homeownership is an appropriate role for the government. Some claim that efforts to promote ownership have had a disastrous effect on the economy. Others believe that homeownership is often unfairly blamed during financial crises and should be encouraged. Indeed, a historical review of government efforts to promote homeownership reveals conflicting views that are reflective of the current housing-crisis debate.

One of the first government efforts to promote homeownership was instituted by then-secretary of commerce Herbert Hoover in the early 1920s, who would later become US president shortly before the stock market crash of October 1929 and the subsequent Great Depression. Hoover inaugurated the Own Your Own Home campaign, writing in 1925 that "the present large proportion of families that own their own homes is both the foundation of a sound economic and social system and a guarantee that our society will continue to develop rationally as changing conditions demand."[4] Though a conservative Republican, Hoover held progressive views and believed that government, working with the private sector, should promote homeownership in the country. Indeed, during his tenure as commerce secretary, ownership of homes increased from 45.6 percent in 1920 to 47.8 percent in 1930.

Although the causes of the Great Depression of the 1930s are complex and debated to this day, some claim that even before the Great Depression, foreclosures were rising. According to critics, such as Steven Malanga of the conservative Manhat-

4. Ibid.

tan Institute, these foreclosures were a result of Hoover's policies promoting homeownership. He argues that Hoover's Own Your Own Home campaign encouraged American homeowners to take on mortgages that were beyond their reach. When the stock market crashed in October 1929, panicked bank depositors withdrew money, and the banks ran out of capital. Thus, those homeowners with short-term mortgages that required refinancing could not get new loans. As a result, many homes went into foreclosure, with as many as one thousand homes a day being repossessed by banks in 1933. Not unlike the housing crisis of today, in addition to homeowners and financial institutions, construction and other related industries suffered, leading to more job loss. Present-day critics, such as Malanga, who blame government policies that promote homeownership for the housing crisis then and now, believe the housing debacle during the Great Depression should have discouraged further federal involvement in promoting homeownership. However, the policies of Democrat Franklin D. Roosevelt, who succeeded Hoover as US president, would increase government involvement and forever change home financing in the United States.

During his first year in office, Roosevelt created the Home Owners' Loan Corporation to help struggling homeowners transfer their loans to long-term mortgages. The agency purchased at-risk mortgages and refinanced them with better terms. The Federal Housing Administration (FHA), created in 1934, offered insurance to lenders who offered low-risk mortgages. As this lowered the risk of lending, banks were able to offer homebuyers better and longer terms. As a result, the twenty- to thirty-year mortgage that covered 80 percent of the cost of a home became the standard loan agreement in the residential real estate market. This revolutionized the housing market and made it possible for middle-class Americans to buy homes. In addition, to encourage further support of long-term loans, and thus mortgage lending and homeownership, the Federal National Mortgage Association (Fannie Mae), created in 1938, purchased long-term loans from lenders to give these businesses the cash they needed to offer more loans. In turn, Fannie Mae would convert these long-term mortgages into securities, which it traded on the stock exchange to raise more funds. These institutions, combined with mortgages insured by the Veterans Administration (VA) created by the G.I. Bill following World War II, did indeed create a post-war boom that increased homeownership from 43.6 percent in 1940 to 61.9 percent in 1960.

Although this boom created what Cannato calls a home-owning middle class and in fact drove the post-war economic boom, these policies were not beloved by everyone. Then housing advocate Charles Abrams feared that efforts to promote homeownership would lure low-income families into high-risk loans. In a 1946 article, "Your Dream Home Foreclosed," Abrams argued that economic stability was not dependent on the number of families who owned homes but on "how sound the ownership is."[5] Sociologist John Dean also anticipated a housing crisis in his 1945 book, *Home Ownership: Is it Sound?* Although his fears would not materialize until decades later, Dean warned that "America will no doubt look back on our time as an era in which society encouraged its families to stride ahead through a field deliberately sown with booby traps."[6]

The next big push in government-promoted homeownership came as an effort to rectify discrimination against minority homeownership. In order to insure mortgages, the FHA set strict standards based on a geographical rating system that determined whether the homes were a worthwhile investment and its residents creditworthy. Those neighborhoods that received the highest ratings were typically populated by well-off

5. As quoted in Steven Malanga, "Obsessive Housing Disorder," *City Magazine*, Spring 2009. http://www.city-journal.org/2009/19_2_homeownership.html.
6. As quoted in Cannato, op. cit.

whites and those that received the lowest ratings were populated by low-income racial and ethnic minorities. According to Cannato, a 1930s FHA manual listed "infiltration of inharmonious racial or national groups" as high risk. During the 1960s, an era of civil rights struggles and urban riots, lawmakers from both parties believed that homeownership would stabilize communities and stem the tide of unrest. Then Democratic congressman Wright Patman reasoned, "Past experience has shown that families offered decent homes at prices they can afford have demonstrated a new dignity,"[7] while Republican senator Charles Percy argued, "People won't burn down houses they own."[8]

Thus, in 1965 Congress created the Department of Housing and Urban Development (HUD). The department urged the FHA to give low-income urban residents heavily subsidized mortgages. The program, known as Section 235, faced challenges from the outset. Real estate speculators created fear that poor minorities using these loans would overtake white neighborhoods. This led to panic selling, and the speculators who purchased the properties sold them to minorities at inflated prices valued by corrupt appraisers. Foreclosures increased and HUD now owned thousands of worthless properties. Following a congressional investigation, the program was shut down. Although some blame the corruption of real estate speculators for the program's failure, others, such as Harvard University historian Louis Hyman, remarked, "The program could not work because it tried to solve a problem of wealth creation through debt creation."[9] For Hyman and like-minded analysts, homeownership creates debt, not wealth, and thus does nothing to alleviate the minority wealth gap.

Although policy makers from both parties continued efforts to close the gap between white and minority homeown-

---

7. As quoted in Malanga, op. cit.
8. Ibid.
9. Ibid.

ership during the 1970s and 1980s, the administration of Bill Clinton pursued an even broader homeownership agenda. "I want to target new markets, underserved populations, tear down the barriers of discrimination wherever they are found,"[10] said Clinton at a 1994 meeting of the National Association of Realtors. Clinton believed that if the FHA and Fannie Mae effectively opened lending to the middle class after World War II, these institutions could help lower-income Americans become homeowners as well. The Clinton administration encouraged both Fannie Mae and its competitor, Freddie Mac, the Federal Home Loan Mortgage Corporation, to buy and trade securities for mortgages that originated with low- and moderate-income borrowers. At first HUD encouraged Fannie and Freddie to trade up to 40 percent of its mortgages from low-income borrowers, but later HUD pushed this target to 50 percent. However, since Fannie Mae and Freddie Mac did not originate loans, but only bought and traded them, the organizations encouraged banks and other lenders to make loans to low-income home buyers on liberal terms based on the promise that they would receive better terms from Fannie and Freddie once the loans were resold. One lender that aggressively participated in this program was Countrywide Financial, a name that has become synonymous with the excesses that led to the current housing crisis. Countrywide offered increasingly liberal terms to risky buyers, including no down payment, interest-only payments, and short-term adjustable rate mortgages. Although there were those who saw the risks in such practices and called for caution, such as James Johnson, Fannie Mae's CEO at the time, the government continued to pressure Fannie Mae to continue buying these risky loans.

When George W. Bush became president in 2001, he continued to make homeownership a key priority. He hoped to create an "ownership society," language he regularly used in

10. As quoted in Cannato, op. cit.

public speeches. Bush wanted to create 5.5 million more minority homeowners by 2010, and his administration increased Fannie Mae's target for purchasing and trading low-income mortgages to 56 percent. According to Cannato, "Lenders kept lending, granting increasingly sizable mortgages and increasingly generous terms to increasingly risky borrowers."[11] More and more borrowers had little to no equity on their homes. Nevertheless, as housing prices rose and artificially low interest rates continued, homeowners paid little attention to their mortgages or their debts, expecting to refinance their loans at a later date as their homes appreciated in value. At the time, Cannato claims, most analysts thought this provided liquidity and spread the risk over the market. Indeed, homeownership had hit an all-time high of 69 percent by 2004.

When the housing bubble burst in 2006, however, many of these homeowners held mortgages greater than the value of their homes, and foreclosures exploded. This significantly hurt banks and investors who held securities on these failed mortgages and the entire economy suffered. While some blame the policies of Clinton and Bush, Cannato reasons that "like many others before them, they assumed with little evidence that home ownership would be a panacea."[12] Malanga agrees, "The ideal of homeownership has become so sacrosanct, it seems, that we never learn."[13] In an effort to explain the problem, Cannato points out what he believes to be the inherent contradiction in federal housing policy, which "became something like a dog chasing its own tail. Encouraging home ownership would drive prices up, but the more expensive homes got, the more difficult it became to enter the housing market, driving the government to loosen lending standards and let more buyers into the market. The cycle continued and the bubble

11. op. cit.
12. op. cit.
13. op. cit.

grew."[14] Thus, Cannato states, "it is time to declare a morato-
rium on new federal programs intended to encourage home
ownership."[15]

Other commentators claim, however, that blaming the
principle of homeownership is unfair, as the culprit was not
the policies that encouraged people to own their own homes
but the bankers whose greed led them to push "low-quality
mortgages on any applicant who could hold a pen. And it was
those risky products—bristling with hidden fees, prepayment
penalties, exposure to variable interest rates—not risky borrowers, that produced the crisis,"[16] argues *Los Angeles Times*
columnist Michael Hiltzik. Policy makers should not blame
homeowners and discourage homeownership. "Homeownership is a goal that should be encouraged by government policy.
Homeowners vote more often than renters. They engage more
with neighborhood and community groups. Studies suggest
that their children do better in school and are more likely to
graduate from high school and move on to postsecondary
education,"[17] Hiltzik concludes.

Clearly, whether the government should promote homeownership remains hotly contested, as the divergent view-
points in *At Issue: The American Housing Crisis* make clear.
The authors of this volume debate the nature and scope of
America's housing crisis, its causes, and policies that will best
address it. Despite his concerns about government housing
policy, Cannato concludes, "No matter what the federal government does, the desire to own a home will continue to burn
in most Americans' hearts. That desire is an inseparable piece
of the larger American Dream, and it generally makes good,
practical, social, and economic sense."[18] However, he cautions,

14. op. cit.
15. op. cit.
16. Michael Hiltzik, "Homeownership Remains a Goal That Should Be Encouraged," *Los Angeles Times*, August 27, 2013. http://articles.latimes.com/2013/aug/27/business/la-fi-hiltzik-20130828.
17. Ibid.
18. op. cit.

"It is simply not rational to expect that the line on the homeownership chart can or should keep rising until it reaches 100%."[19] Whether policy makers will heed his caution remains to be seen.

19. op. cit.

1

The American Housing Crisis Threatens Families and Neighborhoods

Kevin Zeese and Margaret Flowers

Kevin Zeese, an activist attorney, and Margaret Flowers, a pediatrician, are cohosts of a progressive Washington, DC, talk show and codirectors of It's Our Economy, an organization that encourages citizen participation in economic decision-making and advocates reducing the power of large corporations and banks.

The housing crisis is not over. Foreclosures continue to reduce the wealth of homeowners and their neighbors, particularly in minority communities. Financial institutions created the "fake" recovery since 2008 to create scarcity and inflate home prices. To protect citizens from unscrupulous bankers, local governments should use strategies such as increasing the cost of foreclosures or proclaiming eminent domain, thereby reducing the number of foreclosed and abandoned houses in their communities. Such strategies should allow homeowners to remain in their homes until banks come up with better solutions than foreclosure. In addition, policy makers should devise a principal reduction strategy that does not require the approval of a dysfunctional Congress. Indeed, to diffuse the anger of an increasingly frustrated middle class, lawmakers must put the needs of homeowners over banks.

Kevin Zeese and Margaret Flowers, "For Real Economic Recovery, Government Must Stop Favoring Banks Over Homeowners," Truth-out.org, May 29, 2013. First appeared on Truthout.org on May 29, 2013 at http://www.truth-out.org/news/item/16631 -housing-crisis-continues-government-favors-banks-over-people. Reprinted with permission.

We're now in the sixth year [2013] of the economic collapse and the home foreclosure crisis persists. It continues to drag down families, destroy wealth, weaken communities and prevent economic recovery. Inadequate government response has led to a long-term economic crisis that could have been avoided. With good policy, more losses can still be avoided and the economy can begin a real recovery. According to a 2010 report by the Center for Responsible Lending, 2.5 million homes completed the foreclosure process between 2007 and 2010. The 2011 report by the Center for Responsible Lending found that the country was not even halfway through the foreclosure crisis. In total, the Federal Reserve estimates that $7 trillion in home equity was lost from American households between 2006 and 2011 due to the housing crisis.

The crisis of foreclosure and lost wealth is not over. Every three months, 250,000 new families enter the foreclosure process. According to a May 2013 report of the Congressional Budget Office (CBO), more than 13 million homes are still underwater, which increases the risk of foreclosure.

This crisis could have been averted through government policy that placed the needs of people, rather than those of the bankers, first. Because that hasn't happened yet, people are coming together and demanding that the Department of Justice (DOJ) start holding the big banks accountable. The Home Defenders League, a coalition of local groups that are fighting foreclosure, held a series of actions at the DOJ last week.

In this article, we describe what individuals can do to protect themselves and what local and federal governments can do to resolve the foreclosure crisis and place the nation on a path of economic recovery for everyone, not just for the wealthy.

The Foreclosure Crisis and Fake Recovery Hurt Everyone

Homes are the most valuable asset of American workers. Each foreclosure results in an average of $131,200 in lost wealth for the homeowner. In 2012, a total of $192.6 billion in wealth was lost due to foreclosures across the United States. For each of the nation's 113.7 million households, that equals an average of $1,679 in lost wealth. If the 13 million homes still at risk are foreclosed, another $221 billion in wealth will be destroyed, according to a report by the Home Defenders League released on May 20, 2013, "Wasted Wealth: How the Wall Street Crash Continues to Stall Economic Recovery and Deepen Racial Inequity in America."

Foreclosures do not only destroy the wealth of the families who lost their homes; they also drag down neighbors and communities. A report, "The Municipal Cost of Foreclosures," shows that foreclosures can result in as much as an additional $220,000 in reduced property value and home equity for nearby homes. In addition, foreclosure can add costs to local governments. One foreclosure can impose up to $34,000 in direct costs on local government agencies, including inspections, court actions, police and fire department time, potential demolition, unpaid water and sewage, and trash removal. Foreclosures in Newark, New Jersey, have cost the city, and taxpayers, $56 million, according to a report by New Jersey Communities United.

The supposed recovery has been more smoke and mirrors than real.

The foreclosure crisis has been most devastating in poor communities of color. A July 2011 Pew Research analysis found the median wealth among Hispanic households fell by 66 percent and among African-American households it fell by 53 percent after the bursting of the housing market bubble in 2006 and the recession that followed. According to "Wasted Wealth," these were the people who were specifically targeted with sub-prime and high-risk loans—mortgages designed to fail. Communities in which people of color were the majority of residents saw an average of $2,198 in lost wealth per household, while people in predominantly white communities lost an average of $1,267 per household. This massive loss came from a corrupt banking industry pervaded with fraud which targeted these communities.

This massive loss of wealth for working Americans comes in the context of a deep and sustained unemployment crisis that has resulted in tens of millions of Americans giving up trying to work or struggling with long-term unemployment. And for many of those who do work, it has meant lower wages and underemployment. But that is just the most recent crisis.

The US middle class has been in a long period of decline as we experience a race to the bottom in the treatment of workers, combined with a culture of endless consumerism and easy credit, leading to high debts. At present, 52 percent of Americans live paycheck to paycheck, 43 percent spend more than they earn and 46 percent do not have $5,000 in savings. And this is also the result of a so-called "recovery" in which 121 percent of income growth since the economic crash in 2008 has gone to the richest 1 percent of Americans while the remaining 99 percent lost income.

The supposed recovery has been more smoke and mirrors than real. Over the last three years, the total national growth has been 6.3 percent, the slowest growth after an economic collapse compared to all 11 recessions since World War II. This is stagnation, not recovery. The housing market "recovery" being reported currently is a complete hoax created by the Federal Reserve's very low interest rates, which allow investors to borrow money cheaply to buy low-priced houses. The banks have kept 7 million houses in foreclosure off the market in order to create housing scarcity and raise prices. Actual families, who have lost wealth and income and cannot borrow easily, are unable to buy. The manipulation of the housing market is another way the wealthy are stealing wealth from the rest of us. . . .

Using Eminent Domain

There are ways that a local government that is motivated to protect its citizens, communities and city can respond to the foreclosure crisis. One power that has been discussed by dozens of cities—but not yet used—is eminent domain. Eminent domain enables municipal, state or federal governments to take property, which includes mortgages, for a public purpose. As Home Defenders League reports, the use of eminent domain to create the conditions for new sustainable mortgages at current home values while keeping homeowners in their homes serves the public interest.

The way it would work is for the government to condemn underwater mortgages for causing community harm and then issue new mortgages at rates consistent with real housing values. The city would allow the current homeowners to stay in their home. The mortgage holder would be put on notice and required to prove they own the mortgage debt, which is often difficult to do. If they are unable to do so, the lien on the property can be extinguished—leaving the property owned free and clear. If they can show they own the mortgage, then under a condemnation, the investors have the chance to contest in court the compensation they receive to ensure their rights. This threat has been discussed in cities and counties. San Bernardino, California, came the closest to using eminent domain but received threats from lenders which scared them away from it.

The threat of taking property by eminent domain could be coupled with an aggressive program to discourage lenders from abusing borrowers and instead encouraging them to find solutions with homeowners. In Los Angeles, the city attorney has taken the lead on making foreclosure expensive so lenders think twice about foreclosure or abandoning property. City attorney Carmen Trutanich has sued banks over blighted and abandoned homes and their costs to the city. The suits accused mortgage holders of allowing the homes to deteriorate into slums with hundreds of homes falling into disrepair. They also challenged 1,500 foreclosures. The city is seeking to have vacant properties cleaned up and to hold lenders responsible for the impact of loans that have gone bad.

Underwater homeowners are paying housing bubble prices even though the falsely inflated bubble has burst.

Some cities have put fines in place for requiring registration of vacant properties and ensuring they do not become dilapidated. For example, Newark, New Jersey, has a vacant property registration ordinance requiring registration and maintenance of vacant properties. Cities should enact such laws and fully enforce them to bring in revenue and make vacancy and abandonment expensive. These ordinances should be designed to cover all vacant homes and cover the full cost of property vacancy problems to ensure that those responsible for the foreclosure crisis pay the cost.

These kinds of actions begin to change the dynamic by giving banks an incentive to avoid homes becoming vacant or falling into disrepair. By negotiating with homeowners, the banks avoid being sued or fined by the city, or worse, having their mortgage condemned.

Instituting a Principal Reduction Program

One of the solutions recommended in "Wasted Wealth," is to institute a national policy of principal reduction. Underwater homeowners are paying housing bubble prices even though the falsely inflated bubble has burst. As a result, banks continue to profit from the high housing bubble prices created by their corrupt mortgage practices, and homeowners continue to suffer. A strategy of principal reduction would produce an average annual savings of $7,710 ($640 per month) for each underwater homeowner nationwide, boost the US economy by $101.7 billion, and create 1.5 million jobs.

Principle reduction would also bring benefits to those holding the mortgage loans. According to a Chicago Federal Reserve Board report, even investors that own distressed mortgages would stand to save significantly on the expensive costs foreclosures bring. The average foreclosure costs the lender $50,000. "For the lender, foreclosure means absorbing the full loss for outstanding principal, accrued interest, legal fees, costs of holding and maintaining the property, and real estate broker fees, less any amount recovered through the sale of the property." For loan servicers, the economic stream stops when homeowners stop paying their mortgage.

The corruption of the executive and legislative branches in Washington, DC by the big banks has resulted in weak foreclosure and housing policies.

"Wasted Wealth" recommends that Congress, the Obama administration and federal officials take action to "keep people in their homes and preserve community wealth by resetting mortgages." The federal government controls $5 trillion in mortgage assets, but Fannie Mae and Freddie Mac have blocked principle reduction.

Solutions That Recognize Congressional Dysfunction

We recognize the dysfunction in Congress, so we prefer to focus on steps the Obama administration can take without Congress. "Wasted Wealth" points to the following:

- Ensure that Fannie and Freddie and servicer practices discourage foreclosures and place principal reduction at the top of the list of options for helping distressed homeowners.

- After exhausting all loan modification options, including resetting mortgage principal, ensure that

Fannie and Freddie make it a priority to keep families in foreclosed homes through rental or buy-back programs and turn vacant homes over to affordable housing development and community control, not to sources of new speculation and profit-taking by Wall Street speculators.

• Hold Wall Street executives and banks legally accountable for their actions and ensure that future settlements with lenders and servicers are commensurate with the real damage done.

• Use the power of the Treasury, regulatory agencies, and law enforcement to ensure that promised relief (Home Affordable Modification Program, Hardest Hit Funds, National Mortgage Settlement, Independent Foreclosure Review, etcetera) actually reaches families and communities in need of help, starting with the communities of color and neighborhoods targeted for the most abusive lending practices. As a first step, the demographic and geographic data about who receives benefits from programs intended to aid homeowners should be tracked and made public.

• End the practice of allowing the perpetrators of mortgage and foreclosure abuses to administer settlements and ensure that they adhere to fair lending practices.

Putting People's Needs Before Bank Profits

The corruption of the executive and legislative branches in Washington, DC by the big banks has resulted in weak foreclosure and housing policies that have shifted wealth to the wealthiest while destroying the already limited wealth of working families. These policies would have been very different if the government had put people's needs before corporate profits.

President Obama filled his economic team with Wall Street advisers and put Timothy Geithner, who was head of the New York Federal Reserve when the economic crash occurred, in charge of Treasury. Barofsky, the TARP [Troubled Asset Relief Program] inspector, charged that Geithner focused less on the needs of homeowners and more on protecting bank profits. For example, Geithner said TARP funds were to "foam the runway for the banks," that is, lengthen the foreclosure process to spread out the coming wave of foreclosures, rather than refinance mortgages to protect homeowners, many of whom were ripped off by the big banks. Barofsky makes the point that TARP benefitted a single company, American Express, more than all struggling US homeowners combined. "Helping the banks, not homeowners, did in fact seem to be Treasury's biggest concern," Barofsky said in his book, *Bailout*.

The government and the big banks have colluded to deprive the people and the overall economy of what is needed.

Current TARP Special Inspector General Christy L. Romero said in 2012 that just 3 percent of TARP funds that were specifically designated for homeowners in the communities hit hardest by the crisis had been dispersed. She explained to *The New York Times*: "TARP wasn't supposed to be just a bank bailout. It was specifically designed with the goal of helping homeowners, and our concern is that that goal may not be met." She also faults the Obama administration, specifically Geithner's Treasury Department. The banks got the TARP money quickly, but homeowners are still waiting.

On top of receiving $700 billion in TARP money, as of March 2009, $7.77 trillion in low-cost loans were given to the banks by the Fed with no strings attached, at nearly zero percent interest. To this day, through qualitative easing, banks are getting $85 billion a month in low-interest money from the Fed. As noted above, this is leading to a fake housing "recovery" as investors seek to profit from low-cost housing while millions of homeowners still struggle.

Growing Anger

Last week, the anger began to boil over as scores of people who have lost their homes or are struggling to keep them protested the DOJ's failure to prosecute the big banks. Days of protests included occupying the DOJ overnight and blocking the streets and entrances to the building, to which police reacted with arrests and Tasers. They also protested at Covington and Burling, the corporate law firm where Attorney General Eric Holder was a partner and where the head of the DOJ Criminal Division, Lanny Breuer, went after admitting to Frontline that there was no intent at DOJ to prosecute the big banks. Breuer will now receive an estimated $4 million annually from Covington and Burling.

Let's hope the anger of the people continues to show itself. The government and the big banks have colluded to deprive the people and the overall economy of what is needed. The needs of big banks are protected rather than the needs of millions of families who have been thrown out of their homes and the communities which are now in decay. This will change if the people continue to rise up and demand accountability and solutions that place people before profits.

2

Homeownership Is an Unreliable Wealth-Building Strategy

Dennis Ventry

Dennis Ventry is a tax law professor at the University of California, Davis, who regularly comments on tax law and economic policy in newspapers and periodicals.

Claims that homeownership provides social and financial benefits are flawed. No evidence proves that homeowners have better lives than those who rent. In truth, other investment strategies provide greater returns. Indeed, most Americans have more mortgage debt than equity. Housing policies that promote homeownership distort the allocation of capital, increasing the cost of homes. This, in turn, makes owning a home difficult or risky for many. Furthermore, promoting homeownership creates an immobile labor force that increases unemployment. In truth, tax policies, such as the mortgage interest deduction, benefit upper-income not middle-class households. Clearly, policies that promote homeownership do not build wealth or improve the American economy.

Homeownership promises more than it delivers. Americans purchase homes for perceived financial security and social benefits, while politicians push homeownership for

Dennis Ventry, "Homeownership Myths Have Now Been Fully Debunked," *Sacramento Bee*, August 12, 2012. From The Sacramento Bee, August 12, 2012. © 2012 The McClatchy Company. All rights reserved. Used by permission and protected by the Copyright Laws of the United States. The printing, copying redistribution, or retransmission of this Content without express written permission is prohibited.

imagined economic growth. Such claims are traded like stock tips around water coolers and repeated by "experts" paid by the real estate and home building industries. But they are merely myths, widely held but false.

The Myths of Homeownership

Here are some of the biggest whoppers.

• Homeownership is a good investment.

According to housing guru Robert Shiller, from 1950 to 2000, annualized returns to housing averaged less than 0.5 percent after adjusting for inflation.

Returns were even lower over a longer horizon, with real prices growing 0.4 percent per year from 1890 to 2004. Relative to other investments, owner-occupied housing has grossly underperformed.

Between 1926 and 2009, compounded annual returns for small stocks (11.9 percent), large stocks (9.8), long-term government bonds (5.4), and Treasury bills (3.7) far outpaced housing returns.

• Owning a home is the path to prosperity.

At best, homeownership amounts to a decent savings account, but even then it is ineffective. Policies like the mortgage interest deduction encourage taxpayers to finance homes with debt, and result in leveraged ownership, not true ownership.

Between 1950 and 2010, the percentage of home equity plunged from 80 percent to 38.5 percent. In the words of one commentator, "the cold, unsentimental fact about the American dream is that Americans never really owned it in the first place."

• Homeownership creates positive social benefits.

The housing industry likes to say that homeowners enjoy better lives than renters. It touts studies correlating homeownership with higher rates of civic participation, beneficial effects on children's well-being and behavior, and lower rates of crime.

But no study has identified a causal connection between homeownership and what economists call "social capital." Children of homeowners might exhibit lower rates of truancy than children of renters, but that doesn't mean renting will land your kid in juvenile hall or that owning will get her into Harvard.

In fact, studies that isolate causal influences of homeownership on social capital find that the purported benefits disappear and even become negative.

Subsidized mortgage debt encourages homebuyers to consume bigger, costlier homes. Yet artificially boosting the cost of housing helps no one.

• Housing subsidies lower the cost of homeownership.

Current housing policies distort the allocation of financial capital by altering the decision to pay for homeownership with debt over cash or other assets.

Thanks particularly to the mortgage interest deduction, mortgage indebtedness soared in the decade preceding the housing collapse, rising as a percentage of GDP from 47 percent in 1995 to 81 percent by 2007.

Subsidized mortgage debt encourages homebuyers to consume bigger, costlier homes. Yet artificially boosting the cost of housing helps no one. Higher prices prevent millions of potential homebuyers from entering the market.

And while current homeowners may prefer inflated prices for maximizing gain upon sale, any perceived benefit is illusory as sellers become buyers in the same overheated market.

Providing Little Help

• Housing subsidies help the economy.

Housing subsidies distort the decision over where to invest as much as how to invest. By lowering the cost of owner-occupied housing, subsidies contribute to overinvestment in residential real estate.

"Don't build a factory, build a mansion," economist Kevin Hassett has said of the mortgage interest deduction's influence on capital investment. Indeed, while the tax rate on corporate investment exceeds 30 percent, housing enjoys a rate near zero.

The distortions caused by tax subsidies for housing may account for half of all misallocated capital in the economy, shrinking GDP by 10 percent.

They also contribute to labor immobility, which raises unemployment. No wonder nearly every economist believes "the most sure-fire way to improve the competitiveness of the American economy is to repeal the mortgage interest deduction."

• Housing subsidies help middle-class families.

Subsidies for homeownership accrue disproportionately to upper-income households.

Only 3 percent of taxpayers report income over $200,000, but they enjoy 35 percent of the mortgage interest deduction's largesse, while the 75 percent of all taxpayers earning less than $75,000 receive just 11 percent.

In fact, the mortgage interest deduction delivers 10 times the savings for households with income over $250,000 compared to those with income between $40,000 and $75,000.

The disparity in benefits exists because taxpayers receive them only if they itemize deductions.

But just one-third of taxpayers itemize, while two-thirds take the standard deduction (and thus receive no benefits). Even among itemizers, high-income households receive larger benefits, because the value of the subsidy rises as taxable income increases.

There are good reasons to buy a house. But none of them involves attaining financial security, admission to elite colleges, a stronger economy, lower taxes, or the American dream.

3

Can We Afford Another Housing Boom?

Wall Street Journal

The Wall Street Journal *is a daily newspaper that emphasizes business and economic news.*

Although news of a housing revival is certainly good, if government housing subsidies rather than rising prosperity led to the improvement, these policies could create another financial crisis. Homeownership does not create wealth. In truth, the ability to buy a home reflects wealth. Thus, to improve the American economy, the government should invest in technologies that increase productivity and create jobs. The improvement in the housing market should be a reflection of a vibrant economy. Indeed, as housing prices rise, the federal government should reduce housing subsidies and invest in innovation.

Fannie Mae[1] put an exclamation point on the housing rally with last week's announcement of its largest-ever annual profit. The news comes soon after Fannie's cousin, Freddie Mac, announced its own record high. These results may seem like cause for celebration after years of losses at the two

1. Congress chartered The Federal National Mortgage Association (Fannie Mae) and the Federal Home Mortgage Corporation (Freddie Mac) to create a secondary market for residential mortgage loans. Both are considered government-sponsored enterprises (GSEs) because Congress authorized their creation and established their public purpose. Together they are the largest source of housing finance in the United States. They were taken over by the federal government to avert their collapse in September 2008 but have since returned to profitability.

"Can We Afford Another Housing Boom?" *Wall Street Journal*, April 12, 2013. Copyright © 2013 by The Wall Street Journal. All rights reserved. Reproduced by permission.

taxpayer-backed mortgage giants. But they also underscore the urgent need for reform to ensure that the next real estate boom doesn't end as badly as the last one.

It's certainly good news that the very long housing recession is finally over, and that prices in most of the country are rising again. For the 12 months through January, the S&P/Case-Shiller index of 20 U.S. cities shows an annual increase in home prices averaging 8.1%. Prices in Miami were up almost 11% on the year, the Las Vegas market enjoyed a pop of more than 15%, and in Phoenix prices jumped more than 23%. Not a single one of the 20 metropolitan areas in the index suffered an annual price decline.

The healthy part of this revival is the normal adjustment of supply and demand after a painful recession. Foreclosures have been slowly working their way through the system, and the long dry spell in building means there are fewer new homes to buy.

But there's a less desirable side to this new boom: It is fueled by the same kind of government super-subsidy for housing that drove the boom and bust a decade ago. Through Fannie, Freddie and the Federal Housing Administration (FHA), the feds now underwrite some 90% of all mortgages.

Meanwhile, the Fed's rock-bottom interest rates and its QE policies are both intended to reflate the housing market. The Fed is buying $40 billion a month in mortgage securities, despite the housing rebound, plus an additional $45 billion in long-term Treasurys to keep mortgage rates low. This makes it cheaper for families to borrow to buy a home. But the Fed's goal is also to keep rates so low that investors will dive back into real estate in a search for yield they can't get from savings accounts or financial investments.

And sure enough, from Georgia to California, investors have been scooping up residential properties, often in foreclosure auctions. As the *Journal* has reported, large private-equity firms such as Blackstone Group and Colony Capital have spent billions of dollars over the last year buying single-family homes.

Mom and Pop are also back buying property for investment returns, rather than for shelter. A software engineer looking to buy a house in California's Orange County as an investment property recently told the *Journal,* "Right now, it just seems like real estate is a good place to put cash."

Every dollar of capital that policy makers drive into housing is a dollar that won't be spent creating the next great innovation in software or medicine or something else.

It's true that many of today's investors are planning to be landlords collecting regular rent, not speculators betting on their ability to execute a quick flip. But the hard part is knowing how much an asset-price rally is rooted in genuinely rising prosperity and how much in government policies that can't last. One danger sign now is that prices are rising much faster than the economy, which isn't sustainable over time.

It's also worth keeping in mind that housing is not the secret sauce of economic prosperity. The anemic 0.4% GDP growth in the fourth quarter of 2012 would have been even worse without a 17.6% surge in real residential fixed investment. But even though the government calls it investment in GDP calculations, housing is substantially a form of consumption. A large home (assuming the occupant can afford it) is a manifestation of wealth, not a creator of it.

Every dollar of capital that policy makers drive into housing is a dollar that won't be spent creating the next great innovation in software or medicine or something else. Over the long haul, the economy grows when people invest in things *other* than housing—specifically in technologies that enhance productivity and allow all of us to achieve higher living standards. Housing does fine when people are employed and wages are rising. In other words, sustainable growth in real-estate values is a symptom of a vibrant economy, not a cause.

In the 2000s, America tried to use a debt-fueled real-estate boom as a substitute for real wealth creation. The Fed's loose money, government endorsement of private credit-ratings agencies and reckless promotion of homeownership created a housing bubble. The bursting of this bubble created a financial crisis. We do not want to repeat the experience.

Yet there are signs that the politicians have failed to learn that lesson. Beyond the Fed, the *Washington Post* reported last week that "the Obama administration is engaged in a broad push to make more home loans available to people with weaker credit." The government is pressing banks to press borrowers to take advantage of FHA guarantees and other federal subsidies. That's the same thinking that gave us the Fannie Mae-Countrywide Financial subprime loan machine, the subprime bust and the $187.5 billion failure of Fannie and Freddie.

With prices rising again, now is precisely the time to begin reducing the federal subsidies that encourage over-investment in housing. In some areas of the country Fan and Fred still back mortgages of more than $600,000, while the FHA backs loans of more than $700,000. Reform-minded lawmakers may not be able to stop Fed Chairman Ben Bernanke from dropping money from helicopters, but they can begin reducing the conforming loan limits at Fan, Fred and FHA to put some guardrails around Washington's reckless credit policies.

4

Racist Lending Led Minorities to Suffer More from the Housing Crisis

Leela Yellesetty

Leela Yellesetty is a socialist who often publishes commentary and analysis on the International Socialist Organization website, SocialistWorker.org.

Policies to promote minority homeownership did not lead to the disproportionate impact on minorities during the housing crisis—racist lending practices were the true cause. After the housing bubble burst, several major American banks paid hundreds of millions of dollars to settle allegations of discriminatory practices. Testimony revealed evidence of racist remarks about minority customers and the practice of steering minorities toward higher-rate loans. When the housing market collapsed, minorities were thus more likely to lose their homes—even controlling for income differences. Articles that portray minorities as the beneficiaries of a new housing boom in the wake of foreclosures and falling prices reveal that minorities will once again suffer, as banks exploit them to increase profits.

*B*loomberg *Businessweek* stooped to a disgusting new low with a shockingly racist cover illustration for an article on the revival of the housing market. The illustration features

Leela Yellesetty, "The Racist Face of the Housing Crisis," SocialistWorker.org, March 12, 2013. Copyright © 2013 by SocialistWorker.org. All rights reserved. Reproduced by permission.

caricatures of Blacks and Latinos—"with exaggerated features reminiscent of early 20th century race cartoons," as the *Columbia Journalism Review*'s Ryan Chittum wrote—sitting in piles of cash.

The illustration echoes right-wing commentators who claimed "irresponsible" minority homebuyers borrowing beyond their means were responsible for the 2008 financial collapse. One of the most famous examples of this was Fox News' Neil Cavuto, who said, "I don't remember a clarion call that said, 'Fannie and Freddie are a disaster. Loaning to minorities and risky folks is a disaster.'"

The right wing and even mainstream publications repeated this line of argument ad nauseum in the wake of the crash, taking aim at government programs to encourage minority homebuyers such as the 1977 Community Reinvestment Act.

Borrowers of color ... were more than 30 percent more likely to receive a higher-rate loan than white borrowers, even after accounting for differences in risk.

Steering Minorities Toward Riskier Loans

Of course, this argument is nonsense. The opposite is true: minority homeowners have paid disproportionately in the aftermath of the housing crisis due to the racist predatory lending practices of the big banks. Minorities were systematically charged higher fees and steered into riskier subprime loans even when they would have qualified for prime loans.

In 2011, Bank of America (BoA) agreed to pay out $335 million to settle allegations that Countrywide Financial— which BoA bought in 2008—discriminated against minority borrowers. That constitutes the largest residential fair-lending settlement in history.

According to the Department of Justice, "The odds of a minority applicant being steered into such a [subprime] loan were more than twice as high as those for a non-Hispanic white borrower with a similar credit rating."

Last year [2012], Wells Fargo agreed to pay out $175 million due to similar allegations. According to the *Washington Post*, "The average African American taking out a $300,000 prime loan was charged $2,064 more in broker fees than a similarly qualified white customer. Latino borrowers paid an average of $1,251 more."

"They referred to subprime loans made in minority communities as ghetto loans and minority customers as 'those people have bad credit', 'those people don't pay their bills' and 'mud people,'" wrote former Wells Fargo loan officer Tony Paschal in his affidavit.

Whether or not all individual loan officers were racist, the overall pattern was endemic across the banking industry during the housing boom. As early as 2006, the Center for Responsible Lending found that "borrowers of color . . . were more than 30 percent more likely to receive a higher-rate loan than white borrowers, even after accounting for differences in risk."

A Predictable Result

The predictable result was that when the housing bubble burst, minority [borrowers] were disproportionately affected. Again, according to the Center for Responsible Lending, African American borrowers were 76 percent more likely, and Latino borrowers 71 percent more likely, to have lost their homes to foreclosure than white borrowers. These disparities hold even when controlling for differences in income.

The report went on to estimate the "spillover" losses due to depreciating values of nearby properties in communities of color at upwards of $371 billion between 2009 and 2012 alone.

All this has accelerated the trend of a yawning wealth gap between whites and people of color. According to a recent study from the Institute on Assets and Social Policy at Brandeis University, the wealth gap between white and African American families has nearly tripled between 1984 and 2009. More than 25 percent of the gap is directly attributable to homeownership and other policies associated with housing.

According to the Pew Research Center, between 2005 and 2009, Latino wealth fell by 66 percent and Black wealth fell by 53 percent, compared with 16 percent for whites.

An Unforgivable Racist Caricature

Even absent these damning statistics, the *Bloomberg Business-week* cover illustration would have been horribly offensive given the history of racist caricatures of people of color. In light of them, it's unforgivable.

Yet the artist contracted to illustrate the cover, Andres Guzman, claims he had no racist intention. Originally a native of Peru (though he now lives in Colorado), Guzman told Slate's Matt Yglesias, "I simply drew the family like that because those are the kind of families I know. I am Latino and grew up around plenty of mixed families."

Given recent history, it should be clear who will pay the price if yet another housing bubble emerges and then inevitably bursts.

Even if we give the artist the benefit of the doubt as to his intentions, the fact remains that no one on the (all-white and -male) editorial board saw a problem with sending it to print.

After the ensuing uproar, editor Josh Tyrangiel issued the following non-apology: "Our cover illustration last week got strong reactions, which we regret. Our intention was not to incite or offend. If we had to do it over again we'd do it differently." Note that Tyrangiel regrets the strong reactions, not the actual decision to run the cover.

Failing to Explore Who Will Pay the Price

Actually, the article that the cover was meant to illustrate doesn't mention race at all. Instead, it's a perversely cheerful piece on the rebound of Phoenix's housing boom—one of the cities that experienced the most dramatic rise and subsequent collapse in 2008.

Now, thanks to a wave of foreclosures, massive price depreciation and wholesale destruction of the local economy, property values and inventories have fallen so low as to encourage new investment—thereby laying the basis for the whole crazy bubble cycle to begin again.

The article states:

> The price of homes in metropolitan Phoenix could rise 8.5 percent this year, according to Zillow's [Stan] Humphries. Anything much higher than that would be worrisome, says nearly every economist who has looked at the city. [Mike] Orr, the Cromford Report publisher, thinks people are still wary. "But knowing Arizona, we'll probably build too much at some point."

Given recent history, it should be clear who will pay the price if yet another housing bubble emerges and then inevitably bursts. Thankfully, there are signs of resistance to this insanity. In cities across the country, housing rights activists are fighting back, occupying homes to stop foreclosures and evictions and putting the banks' predatory lending practices on trial.

It will take nothing short of a national movement of this sort to take on the banks, who as we now well know use every means at their disposal—including the most vile racism—in their tireless pursuit of profit at our expense.

5

Lending Reform Must Not Unnecessarily Limit Access to Mortgage Credit

David M. Abromowitz

David M. Abromowitz is a senior fellow at the Center for American Progress, a progressive public policy research and advocacy think tank. His research focus is housing policy, financing, and community and economic development.

Lending reform laws proposed in the wake of the housing crisis should not limit middle-class access to homeownership. The United States has a history of helping middle-class Americans own homes. Nevertheless, although disproven, some continue to blame government investment in housing for the foreclosure crisis. As a result, some propose policies that would not only limit access to mortgage credit and economic independence but also stifle innovation, education, and job growth. Policies that constrict credit and increase down payment requirements make it difficult for younger and lower-income families to obtain loans. These limits force people with a steady income who want to own homes to remain renters, thus reducing access to the social benefits of homeownership.

For everyone except hardcore policy wonks and mortgage bankers, it's natural for eyes to glaze over reading headlines such as "QM [qualified mortgage] rule commentary cap-

David M. Abromowitz, "Why Arcane Mortgage Rules Matter for the Middle Class," Center for American Progress, February 21, 2013. Copyright © 2013 by Center for American Progress. All rights reserved. Reproduced by permission.

tures CFPB [Consumer Financial Protection Bureau] website." But numerous arcane incremental policy choices currently being made in Washington to reshape our housing-finance system will determine whether working Americans and their children will be able to move into the middle class, build up assets, and avoid greater dependence on entitlements.

Banking and consumer protection agencies . . . must be careful to make choices that protect consumers without limiting safe and stable access to mortgage credit for the middle class.

Homeownership Is a Path to the Middle Class

Access to homeownership has long been a key component of a family's ability to build wealth in America. In 2010 the equity in one's primary home accounted for 29.5 percent of all family assets in the United States. For those families in the middle-income tiers—neither wealthy nor poor, with annual household incomes between roughly $30,000 and $70,000— home equity represented 40 percent to 50 percent of family wealth. And that was at a time when housing values had fallen dramatically after the U.S. housing bubble burst.

While homeownership is not the only path to building assets—and more needs to be done to create widespread equity options for renters—it remains one of the key underpinnings of broadening the base of prosperity.

Historically, homeowners have built wealth in part because each monthly mortgage payment pays down a little more principal on the loan, building equity through a regular "forced savings" program. Moreover, for most of the past 75 years, houses have shown long-term modest price appreciation—a realistic expectation for the future if policymakers continue prudent steps to avoid repeating the housing bubble of the mid-2000s.

Promoting Middle-Class Homeownership

The rise of homeownership as a tool to help people enter the middle class was in part a result of post–World War II government policies. Before 1940 the U.S. homeownership rate was just 43.6 percent. But with 4.3 million veterans using zero down payment, low-interest Veterans Administration loans to buy homes between 1944 and 1955, and millions of nonveterans borrowing with help from the Federal Housing Administration, or FHA, the homeownership rate climbed to nearly 62 percent by 1960. Beyond veterans benefits, the liquidity and stability that the FHA and the government-sponsored enterprises Fannie Mae and Freddie Mac provided to the home-mortgage markets by continuing to attract private investment to fund home loans expanded the average household's ability to get a long-term, fixed-rate, and safely underwritten loan to purchase a home.

While some conservative commentators still insist that government involvement in the housing market was responsible for the foreclosure crisis, many analysts have debunked this view time and again. It is true, however, that due to the past five years of widespread foreclosures, the federal government has assumed an even larger role in the market by ultimately guaranteeing repayment to private investors buying mortgage securities, maintaining the flow of credit to housing markets to avoid wider economic collapse.

Policy Choices Will Determine Who Can Become a Homeowner

There is emerging consensus that the current degree of governmental direct involvement in the housing finance market is neither sustainable nor desirable. Yet it is important to maintain access to affordable credit while reducing the government's footprint. As banking and consumer protection agencies implement the host of regulations required by the Dodd-Frank Wall Street Reform and Consumer Protection Act, they must be careful to make choices that protect consumers without limiting safe and stable access to mortgage credit for the middle class.

One key issue, for example, is the size of the down payment required to get a mortgage. One regulation that could significantly impact down payments is the so-called risk retention rule and its qualified residential mortgage, or QRM, exemption that will likely be issued by a group of six federal regulators this spring. In brief, for loans to be "securitized"— packaged in large pools and sold as securities to investors— lenders have to hold back on their books 5 percent of the value of loans that do not meet the soon-to-be-released QRM definition, making it less likely that borrowers will be able to get loans that don't fit this upcoming QRM definition.

The QRM definition will address whether larger down payments of 10 percent to 20 percent of the home purchase price will be required for mortgages to be eligible for securitization, which brings hundreds of billions of dollars of private investment into the U.S. mortgage market each year. Loans that cannot be securitized generally carry higher interest rates.

The Impact of the Risk Retention Rule

QRM rules might seem to be arcane issues of financial-system risk analysis. But a QRM rule that makes lower down payments of 3 percent or 5 percent costly and unattractive to mortgage lenders could prevent a generation of younger workers, as well as lower-wealth communities, including those of color, from attaining homeownership.

The Center for Responsible Lending estimated that a mandatory 10 percent down payment (plus closing costs) would require nearly 20 years of savings for the average American family to buy a home. These higher down payments disproportionately affect the very communities that were most preyed upon during the subprime predatory mortgage-lending wave of the 2000s. Black and Latino households, which tend to have less wealth than white households on average, could pay a down payment of only 10 percent or less in roughly 45 percent of home purchases in 2009, in part because black and Latino households are less likely to receive gifts or use inheritance or proceeds from the sale of previous homes to finance their home purchases.

Unduly narrowing safe and sound access to homeownership perversely undercuts the widely shared goal of broadening each family's ability to achieve a degree of self reliance and economic independence.

What's more, locking so many households out of the market by requiring higher down payments would not have a significant effect on reducing systemic risk, according to a study by the UNC Center for Community Capital. That is because the ability-to-pay rule and its qualified mortgage exemption—another complicated but targeted new regulation that was recently finalized and that will go into effect in January 2014—will already prohibit most of the more toxic and higher-risk lending practices that led to the crisis. The UNC researchers concluded that there would be little benefit—in terms of additional reduction in mortgage defaults—from adding tough down-payment requirements on top of that. In fact, it is likely that excluding so many households from the market will have a negative effect on home values for the long term by significantly reducing demand.

Regulators Should Not Unnecessarily Limit Access to Mortgage Credit

No one is arguing, of course, that every family in America can or should buy a home. But unduly narrowing safe and sound access to homeownership perversely undercuts the widely shared goal of broadening each family's ability to achieve a degree of self reliance and economic independence while minimizing the likelihood of needing direct government assistance.

First, severely narrowing access to the conventional mortgage market will likely mean even greater government involvement in mortgage finance for millions of families. We have seen this over the past few years, as the Federal Housing Administration's share of the number of home-purchase mortgage loans grew from just 4.5 percent in 2006 to more than 25 percent of all loans in 2012. A large number of borrowers during this time period were ones who, in normal times, would have been served by the conventional mortgage market but who could not qualify either for the higher down payments or the very high credit scores lenders have required in recent years.

The FHA has handled this influx of demand well, financing some 4 million home-loan purchases and roughly 2.6 million refinancings since 2008, which served a critical countercyclical role in keeping home prices from plunging even further after the housing bubble burst. But the direct government insurance that the agency provides is a much greater and more direct federal government involvement in the home-loan market than is recommended by most proposals for a reformed government catastrophic insurance role in the broader mortgage market.

Forcing People to Remain Renters

Second, unduly restricting access to mortgage credit will force even those who have steady incomes and desires to be homeowners to remain renters. Their monthly payments will build equity for their landlord but not for their family. And the wealth gap between homeowners and renters is already vast: From 2001 to 2010 U.S. homeowners had on average a net worth of $211,150, while renters averaged just $5,250.

Third, in many rental markets, paying rent results in a higher risk of needing other public assistance. One-quarter of U.S. renters now spend more than half of their monthly income on housing, and that percentage isn't expected to go down anytime soon. The National Association of Realtors estimates that average rents will increase nationally by 4.6 percent in 2013 and continue to increase by at least 4 percent per year in 2014 and 2015.

Overly tightening access to homeownership may constrain entrepreneurship, job creation, and educational advancement.

As a result, many workers earning even a decent wage will be unable to build up a personal cushion of savings to call upon in times of economic setback—such as job loss, health issues, death of a loved one, and divorce. This asset drain increases the number of households likely over time to need some form of government assistance in times of economic stress. Research shows, for example, that women without assets are more likely to need welfare assistance following marital disruption than women with assets, who are better able to maintain income and independence.

Constraining Growth

Finally, overly tightening access to homeownership may constrain entrepreneurship, job creation, and educational advancement. Savings in a home have often been a source of capital for entrepreneurship and education. According to a December 2010 study by the Federal Reserve Board of Cleveland, roughly one in four small-business owners in the United States used home equity as a source to finance their businesses before the financial crisis.

The ability to tap home equity has also proven to be a critical factor in access to college. One recent study by Cornell

University researcher Michael F. Lovenheim, after noting that 85 percent of U.S. college attendees come from families that own a home, found that higher amounts of parental home equity increased the likelihood that middle- and lower-class students would enroll in college.

Consequently, both small-business activity and college attendance would likely contract in the future if an unduly large share of American families who are otherwise qualified to be homeowners are locked out of the conventional mortgage market. This will only put greater pressure on governmental sources of financing for small business and higher education.

None of this, as noted earlier, argues for making mortgage loans unduly easy to obtain or overly risky. But the process in Washington that is reshaping the lending rules of the future is moving ahead largely in the language of credit markets, systemic risk analysis, and opaque acronyms such as "QRM"— even though the decisions being made will largely affect Americans outside of Washington and financial circles, vastly reshaping where millions of people will live, what they can save, and whether they can achieve the degree of independence that is central to the American Dream.

6

Dodd-Frank Qualified Mortgage Rules Will Create a New Bubble

Jay Weiser

Jay Weiser is associate professor of law and real estate at Baruch College and author of the upcoming Mercatus Center study "Qualified Mortgage Standards."

Lending reform rules such as the Dodd-Frank Act's Qualified Mortgage provisions will do little to protect against the next housing crisis. These rules do not discourage risk—they simply force lenders to make loans that will not subject them to liability. However, bad lenders alone were not the cause of the housing crisis. The true cause was ignoring long-standing lending practices based on the borrower's ability to pay, the borrower's willingness to pay, and the size of the loan in relation to the property's value. Overly specific regulations designed to protect borrowers force lenders to look for loopholes that in fact encourage risky practices that fuel irresponsible borrowing. Policies that force borrowers to put their own money at risk rather than depending on government subsidies will prevent another housing bubble.

Father Edward Flanagan, the legendary founder of Boys Town, said, "There are no bad boys. There is only bad environment, bad training, bad example, bad thinking." Father

Jay Weiser, "Dodd-Frank Qualified Mortgage Rules Will Create a New Bubble," *US News & World Report*, January 16, 2013. Copyright © 2013 by US News & World Report. All rights reserved. Reproduced by permission.

Flanagan lives on in the Dodd-Frank Act's Qualified Mortgage provisions, which imagine a housing market where there are no bad borrowers, only bad laws and bad lenders who will cease sinning if the catechism (in the form of 804 pages of regulations) is long enough. Perversely, Qualified Mortgage protects lenders from liability for many high-risk loans, encourages riskier loan types, and continues to rely on federal agency guarantees. Dodd-Frank must be simplified to require borrower skin in the game.

The Consumer Financial Protection Bureau's new Qualified Mortgage regulations are meant to assure that residential borrowers only take loans that are suitable for them. But Dodd-Frank's suitability rules are enforced with a sledgehammer, with damages too high for most lenders to risk. Effectively, lenders subject to the regulations will be forced to make only loans under Qualified Mortgage's safe harbor that protect them from liability—or loans that exploit Qualified Mortgage's loopholes.

The safe harbor requirements were only loosely based on empirical evidence of the causes of default. Some requirements, such as bans on negative amortization, interest-only, and no-doc (no borrower income or asset verification) loans, will probably make borrowers less likely to take on risks they don't understand. Limitations on excessive points (fees deducted from the loan amount) will make it more difficult for lenders to disguise high interest rates.

While these features became common at the bubble's peak, they were not core causes of the bust. That came from ignoring lending principles: borrower ability to pay (debt-to-income ratio), borrower willingness to pay (as evidenced by credit score), and the size of the loan relative to the value of the property (loan-to-value ratio). The result was Ponzi finance, in which borrowers took down ever-larger loans in the expectation that rising prices would allow them to refinance out of unaffordable debt. When prices dropped, massive defaults followed. Of these three key criteria, Qualified Mortgage only addresses one: debt-to-income ratio.

[Qualified Mortgage] exemptions are less about protecting unsophisticated borrowers than about protecting the taxpayer-guaranteed business models of favored entities.

Although lenders will find the debt-to-income safe harbor the financial equivalent of Rotterdam's Maeslantkering flood barrier, borrowers may feel like Jersey Shore denizens during Hurricane Sandy.[1] The Qualified Mortgage regulations set the maximum debt-to-income ratio at 43 percent—yet it is unclear that debt-to-income is the relevant measure. As the Consumer Financial Protection Bureau acknowledges, Federal Reserve Board research shows "debt-to-income ratios may not have significant predictive power once the effects of credit history, loan type, and loan-to-value are considered."

The safe harbor itself permits risky loans, but Qualified Mortgage loopholes encourage further risk. Dodd-Frank exempts home equity lines of credit—revolving credit lines, secured by second mortgages—that turned borrowers' homes into ATMs as prices appreciated. The Qualified Mortgage regulations will encourage borrowers to unsustainably leverage up with home equity lines of credit soon after closing, like Bridezillas who go off their crash diets the minute they tie the knot. The home equity lines of credit exemption will also encourage lenders to offer hazardous high-debt-to-income ratio, home equity lines of credit first mortgages. (Timeshare loans and reverse mortgages are also exempt; kudos to their lobbyists.)

---

1. The Maeslantkering, a Netherlands storm surge barrier, is a marvel of engineering designed to automatically protect the community surrounding the port of Rotterdam by closing during extreme weather events yet otherwise remaining open to shipping in one of the busiest ports of the world. The people living in New Jersey shore communities had no such protection and suffered significant losses due to storm surge during Hurricane Sandy in October 2012.

The Consumer Financial Protection Bureau offers further Qualified Mortgage exemptions for government-favored financial services entities that have traded in high-risk, low-cost loans for 40 years, using regulatory arbitrage to drive out market-priced competitors. The regulation exempts loans involving Fannie/Freddie (a $187.5 billion bailout so far) and federal agencies such as the Federal Housing Administration. The Federal Housing [Administration]'s post-bubble binge, Ed Pinto reports, enticed over 300,000 low-income borrowers into unaffordable loans, likely wrecking their credit while leaving the agency $31 billion underwater with a 10 percent default rate. The Consumer Financial Protection Bureau proposes to extend the exemption to community banks (whose savings and loan predecessors went bust on bad housing loans in the 1970s) and nonprofits (which laundered developer loans to low-income borrowers for sham down payments in "down payment assistance" programs, fueling the bubble). These exemptions are less about protecting unsophisticated borrowers than about protecting the taxpayer-guaranteed business models of favored entities.

Despite all the verbiage, Qualified Mortgage does not require borrowers to have skin in the game in the form of substantial equity. The statute and regulations are silent on the loan-to-value ratio. (Other forthcoming regulations will address this indirectly through complex lender risk retention and reserve requirements.) During the bubble, borrowers leveraged up: By 2006, the median down payment for first-time buyers was 2 percent. With artificially low-interest financing courtesy of the Greenspan/Bernanke put and Fannie/Freddie implied guarantee, borrowers went into a refinancing and house-flipping frenzy. They were indifferent to risks, believing that they were making a one-way taxpayer-funded leveraged bet.

The Qualified Mortgage regulations, by giving the lender sole responsibility for suitability, will continue to discourage borrower prudence. Consumer Financial Protection Bureau Director Richard Cordray tells the sob story of Henry, whose house went into foreclosure after his $50,000 salary was insufficient to pay his $500,000-plus mortgage. In Cordray's funhouse mirror world, Henry never chose to borrow this huge amount—the lender "sold him a mortgage." While there is a place for suitability rules, the United States will float from bubble to bubble until borrowers have real money at risk. Investing substantial cash in a house—20 percent down payments were common before the decision to massively subsidize the American Dream—would give borrowers an incentive to examine whether their housing purchases and mortgages make sense, rather than having taxpayers bear the loss.

7

Lending Reform Threatens Minority Homeownership

Liz Peek

Liz Peek, a former Wall Street analyst, writes commentary for The Fiscal Times, The New York Sun, and FoxNews.com. She also appears regularly on Fox News business programs as a financial analyst.

Consumer protection regulations designed to protect American borrowers from risky home loans actually hurt the borrowers they are designed to protect. Bankers have already tightened available credit in the wake of the housing crisis. Unfortunately, fearing liability for loans to low-credit applicants, these bankers further restrict credit, making it difficult for minorities and low-income Americans to obtain loans. Moreover, some experts claim that the restrictions, not higher interest rates, have actually reduced home sales. Indeed, tight credit dampens demand. Thus, mortgage loan restrictions undo years of efforts to expand home-ownership among minorities and low-income Americans, increasing the wealth gap.

Is the government engaged in redlining? Dick Bove, long-time bank analyst now at Rafferty Capital Markets, charges that the Obama administration, in its efforts to prevent another financial crisis, has inadvertently pushed banks to deny credit to minorities in low-income neighborhoods. In the old days, you could be sued for that.

Liz Peek, "New Mortgage Rules Threaten Minority Home Ownership," *Fiscal Times*, January 16, 2013. This column first appeared on January 16, 2013 in The Fiscal Times, which also owns the copyright. Reproduced by permission.

Protecting Americans from Themselves

This incendiary reading of the current state of the mortgage market is not unreasonable. The Consumer Financial Protection Bureau [CFPB] has recently issued new regulations designed to protect Americans from themselves, and the country from another housing bust. The rules define what constitutes "affordability" for a "qualified" mortgage. The affordability test demands that a borrower's total debt payments not exceed 43 percent of income.

Other rules eliminate exotic no-interest and reverse-amortization loans. "Qualified" mortgages are attractive for banks because they can be sold off in their entirety to bundlers without the originator retaining a residual interest ("skin in the game"). Also, banks making "qualified" loans are protected against lawsuits by those who get in over their heads.

In reviewing the new regulations, *The New York Times* was alarmed that banks received such legal protections, but pleased that banks received fewer safeguards on loans made to subprime applicants than they did in lending to so-called "prime" borrowers. Credit-challenged borrowers would be able to take their lender to court without much difficulty; and subprime borrowers would be able to give a judge "oral evidence." That is, they could argue in person that the "bank made them do it." (That's my interpretation—not *The Times*.)

In an accompanying editorial, *The Times* celebrates the new rules, which they say will "help protect home buyers and the global financial system from a repeat of the subprime disaster." However, they are alarmed that the 43 percent limit may not be protective enough. They point out that such a standard is probably sufficient for a family with $100,000 in income; but a family earning only $50,000 might be hard pressed to shell out 43 percent of their income and still put food on the table. They would like to see the standards tightened.

Note that, as is so often the case with those who think the government knows best, *The Times* never suggests that the borrower is responsible for, or capable of, assessing his (or her) own finances.

Policies aimed at protecting [low-income] borrowers are threatening to undo solid progress in this arena.

Cutting Back Lending

As usual when the government intrudes into markets, it is behind the curve. Bankers didn't much resist the new lending rules, because they have already ratcheted up their own guidelines. Lawrence Yun, Chief Economist for the National Association of Realtors [NAR], said at a press conference last fall that it is restrictive loan standards—which now exceed Fannie and Freddie guidelines—that have retarded the rebound in home sales, not excessive interest rates.

In a speech last November [2012], Fed Chief Ben Bernanke said that the "extension of first-lien mortgages to purchase homes fell by more than half from 2006 to 2011 and now stands at the lowest level since 1995." Cautious banks have especially cut back lending to those with low credit scores. According to Bernanke, "the contraction in mortgage originations has been particularly severe for minority groups and those with lower incomes: Since the peak in mortgage lending in 2006, the number of home-purchase loans extended to African Americans and Hispanics has fallen more than 65 percent, whereas lending to non-Hispanic whites has fallen less than 50 percent. Home-purchase originations in lower-income neighborhoods have fallen about 75 percent, compared with around 50 percent for middle- and upper-income neighborhoods."

Bernanke points out that myriad factors have dampened demand for housing, including unemployment and uncertainty about the economy, but he also cites tightened credit as culpable.

Undoing Solid Progress

Uncle Sam has encouraged expanded home ownership among minorities and low-income Americans since 1968 when the Housing and Urban Development Act authorized subsidized mortgages for low-income homebuyers for the first time. Now, policies aimed at protecting such borrowers are threatening to undo solid progress in this arena. To quote Bernanke again, "most or all of the hard-won gains in homeownership made by low-income and minority communities in the past 15 years or so have been reversed. . . . Data from the Census Bureau show that, over the period from 2004 to 2012, the homeownership rate fell about 5 percentage points for African Americans, compared with about 2 percentage points for other groups." All this while the Federal Reserve is spending $40 billion a month to keep mortgage rates low and affordable. Nothing is affordable if credit is out of reach.

Though bankers are understandably eager to avoid further mortgage losses, and therefore unlikely to open the lending floodgates anytime soon to low-credit applicants, creating greater legal vulnerability for doing so is making things worse, not better. Consumer advocates should ask themselves: Will banks be more or less likely to lend to groups that can easily sue them? Will they make loans that require higher capital backing (if they must retain a portion of the loan) or choose those which need no capital and therefore promise greater returns?

The greatest irony is this: CFPB policies will guarantee that it will be the well-to-do who benefit from an expected snap-back in home prices. The NAR's Yun said new, tighter mortgage rules are "limiting who can become home owners and setting the stage for possible highly unequal wealth distribution in five years"—an outcome he described as an "unwelcome social development." I would say so.

8

Refinancing Programs Will Help the Economy and Reduce Foreclosures

John Griffith, Janneke Ratcliffe, and David M. Abromowitz

Janneke Ratcliffe and David M. Abromowitz are housing policy fellows at the Center for American Progress (CAP), a progressive public policy research and advocacy think tank. Former CAP fellow John Griffith is now a senior analyst with Enterprise Community Partners, which offers low-income housing opportunities.

The Barack Obama administration's plans to help responsible homeowners avoid foreclosure will in turn spur America's economic recovery. Programs that help struggling homeowners refinance their mortgages at lower interest rates frees up money that they can then spend on consumer goods. For those homeowners whose home values have dropped so significantly that they cannot refinance even at a low interest rate, modifications that reduce the principal are in many cases less costly for banks than foreclosure. Taxpayer-supported, government-sponsored mortgage finance companies could pass these savings on to the taxpayer. Moreover, some analysts report that principal reduction reduces the loan default rate. Clearly, keeping homeowners in their homes promotes housing stability, which in turn benefits all Americans.

President Barack Obama recently renewed his commitment to struggling homeowners by announcing two major changes to his administration's foreclosure prevention strategy.

John Griffith, Janneke Ratcliffe, and David M. Abromowitz, "Rewarding Homeowners for Good Behavior," Center for American Progress, February 2, 2012. Copyright © 2012 by Center for American Progress. All rights reserved. Reproduced by permission.

If successful, the administration's plans could make a meaningful dent in the ongoing foreclosure crisis but only with the cooperation of Congress and federal regulators.

President Obama's first announcement came in last Tuesday's State of the Union address [delivered on January 24, 2012], when he pledged to give "every responsible homeowner" the chance to refinance his or her mortgage at today's historically low rates. According to details released yesterday, the new program would help millions of homeowners refinance into new mortgages made by private companies and guaranteed by the Federal Housing Administration [FHA], a government-run mortgage insurer. Eligible homeowners must be making timely mortgage payments on the home in which they live and meet other requirements, with a focus on those who are "underwater," owing more than their home is worth.

President Obama yesterday explained that his plan would help "millions of responsible homeowners who make their payments on time but find themselves trapped under falling home values or wrapped in red tape." It would not help "the neighbors down the street who bought a house they couldn't afford then walked away and left a foreclosed home behind," nor would it benefit those who "bought multiple homes just to speculate and make a quick buck," he said.

In a different announcement the Treasury Department late Friday unveiled changes to the Home Affordable Modification Program, or HAMP. Since its creation in 2009, HAMP has helped about 900,000 struggling homeowners with private and government-backed loans make their mortgage more affordable by extending terms, lowering the interest rate, or reducing principal. In response to lower-than-expected uptake in its inaugural years, Treasury extended the program's enrollment deadline, expanded eligibility to more borrowers, and strengthened incentives for servicers and investors to write down mortgage principal.

Together these efforts could help lower monthly housing costs, deleverage household debt, and keep struggling families in their homes, all of which would help our broader economic recovery. But first they'll have to leap a few massive hurdles.

A Closer Look at the President's Refinancing Plan

If designed well, a mass refinancing program like the one the president proposed has enormous potential to spur economic growth. Three out of four underwater borrowers, or roughly 8 million households, are paying above-market interest rates on their mortgages today according to CoreLogic. Each of these families that are still current on their payments can immediately lower their monthly housing bills by refinancing to mortgages at today's market rate. But often private lenders will not let them simply because they're underwater.

Though promising, the president's proposal is guaranteed to hit speed bumps.

The White House estimates the new program will save the average eligible family about $3,000 a year in housing costs, which could in turn be spent on clothes, food, and other consumer goods, spurring new business investments. By comparison that's three times the expected household benefit from extending the payroll tax cut.

The new program would work alongside existing refinancing initiatives for mortgages guaranteed by the federal government, namely FHA's Streamlined Refinancing Program and the newly revamped Home Affordable Refinancing Program, or HARP, which helps homeowners refinance loans owned by the government-controlled mortgage giants Fannie Mae and Freddie Mac.

According to the Federal Reserve, between 1 million and 2.5 million homeowners are current on their mortgage payments and meet all the underwriting standards to refinance under HARP but cannot because their loan is not guaranteed by Fannie or Freddie. That's why the president's proposed program targets creditworthy borrowers with purely private mortgage loans. In addition the White House yesterday called on Congress to make it easier for homeowners with Fannie and Freddie mortgages to refinance through HARP.

Hurdles to Clear

Though promising, the president's proposal is guaranteed to hit speed bumps.

Many borrowers are trying in good faith to keep up with their payments but are too underwater to afford their loan even at today's interest rates. That's where HAMP modifications come in.

For starters, the new refinancing program would require congressional approval—no small feat at a time of strong conservative opposition to further government intervention in the housing market.[1] The president also proposed a "Financial Crisis Responsibility Fee" on the nation's largest financial institutions to cover the program's estimated $5 billion to $10 billion price tag, ensuring the program does not add to the deficit or draw on FHA's existing funds.

But it's unclear whether FHA would need additional congressional authority to collect such a fee. If so, the measure is

---

1. Republications did in fact stall a vote on these proposals. Nevertheless, the Home Affordable Modification Program, known as HAMP, and related consumer protections will remain in effect through 2015. This extension aligns HAMP with other housing relief initiatives that also have been extended. That includes the Home Affordable Refinance Program and the Streamlined Modification Initiative for homeowners whose mortgages are owned or guaranteed by Fannie Mae and Freddie Mac, government-sponsored mortgage companies. As of July 2013, Obama's mass refinancing program has yet to gain full congressional support nor has Fannie and Freddie reduced principal on its mortgages.

especially unlikely to pass this Congress, with its particular aversion to new revenue increases.

Second, some critics have argued that any large-scale refinancing initiative will be unpopular among mortgage investors who have been benefiting from holding these above-market-rate assets. But as Moody's Mark Zandi points out, the expected losses in interest income only "modestly dilute" the overall economic benefit of refinancing. And most of these investors probably should have already been "refinanced out of their investments" by now, Zandi added.

New Incentives for Lenders to Write Down Mortgage Principal

Even if the mass refinancing plan were to pass Congress and win support from investors, it would provide little relief to another major segment of homeowners: those who have just started falling behind on their mortgages. Many borrowers are trying in good faith to keep up with their payments but are too underwater to afford their loan even at today's interest rates. That's where HAMP modifications come in.

In reforming HAMP the administration was wise to focus on principal reduction, which many experts recognize as a necessary but missing piece to existing efforts. To avoid future default lenders recognize lost value on the home and structure a better deal with the existing owner so banks and homeowners share losses from the housing collapse. This in turn reduces foreclosures and helps underwater borrowers dig their way out of debt.

Even though one in four borrowers is currently underwater, fewer than 5 percent of permanent HAMP modifications have featured principal reduction. That's largely because Fannie Mae and Freddie Mac have so far refused to offer principal write-downs as part of their modifications, which cuts out about half of the mortgages in the United States. That makes the Federal Housing Finance Agency, or FHFA—which regulates Fannie and Freddie as their government conservator—a "big boulder in the path to principal reduction," according to former Obama economic advisor Jared Bernstein.

To defend its position FHFA last week released a report demonstrating its slight preference toward principal forbearance, where a lender temporarily defers payments but maintains the total amount owed on the loan. But the report's true takeaway is something many have long touted: Principal reduction yields a positive net value to Fannie and Freddie's books compared to doing nothing.

Partial write-downs will avoid foreclosures and provide stability to the housing market, which benefits the broader economy and financial system.

FHFA's own analysis found that write-downs for all severely underwater borrowers—those that owe at least 15 percent more on their mortgage than their home is worth— would actually *save* Fannie and Freddie—and the taxpayers supporting them—about $20 billion over the life of those loans. Indeed, a principal forbearance plan was projected to save Fannie and Freddie slightly more, but FHFA admits that this difference is probably negligible: "Our conclusion was that while forbearance shows a slightly lower loss than [principal reduction], the difference is negligible given the model risk," the authors wrote.

It's worth noting that many analysts, including the White House's Bernstein, have expressed serious concerns over FHFA's calculations, the details of which were not disclosed in the analysis. But even if you ignore the technical issues, FHFA's analysis still ignores the long-term benefits of principal reduction compared to forbearance.

Where appropriate, partial write-downs will avoid foreclosures and provide stability to the housing market, which benefits the broader economy and financial system, including

Fannie Mae and Freddie Mac. The Federal Reserve in a recent white paper to Congress also described targeted principal reduction as a way to decrease the probability of default, improve migration between labor markets, and make households more resilient to economic shocks.

Similarly, Laurie Goodman of Amherst Securities recently told Congress that principal reduction is "the key to a successful modification" since "negative equity drives defaults." In a separate report Goodman pointed out that write-downs have much lower redefault rates than other modifications, especially for less risky "prime" mortgages.

The bottom line is clear: Focused principal reduction yields positive results for mortgage lenders. That's why more than 15 percent of private modifications involved some principal reduction in the third quarter of 2011 according to the Office of the Comptroller of the Currency. Now it's just a matter of convincing Fannie, Freddie, and FHFA that it's the best option for them.

There's a good chance last week's changes to HAMP could accomplish exactly that. Among other things, the revised HAMP rules extend new incentives to Fannie and Freddie to write down principal. For the first time Fannie, Freddie, and their servicers could get as much as 63 cents on every dollar written off, depending on the riskiness of the loan. It's unclear whether that'll be enough to get FHFA on board, but it's an undeniable step in the right direction.

The administration is wise to focus on commonsense reforms that address the housing overhang slogging our economy. In the coming weeks we'll see whether Congress and federal regulators will join President Obama and move these proposals forward.

9

Laws That Prevent Foreclosures Delay Recovery from the Housing Crisis

Anthony Randazzo and Katie Furtick

Anthony Randazzo is director of economic research and Katie Furtick is a policy analyst at the Reason Foundation, a libertarian think tank.

Despite evidence of a housing recovery, more home foreclosures are likely. These foreclosures will continue to decrease housing prices in many communities. In an effort to slow the number of foreclosures, a new Massachusetts law requires lenders to prove that they in good faith tried to help delinquent borrowers. Unfortunately, the law includes terms that are difficult for judges to define and interpret. Moreover, these laws require that judges, who are not qualified to make such determinations, decide whether a lender is more likely to profit from foreclosure than from a mortgage modification. Thus, judges may unknowingly keep banks that make false estimates in business, while putting honest lenders at risk. Such processes unnecessarily slow the process of foreclosure and thus artificially delay real housing recovery.

With a large amount of housing data coming out over the next few days (including the FHFA price data leaked last night [October 23, 2012]), we are likely to see a full range

Anthony Randazzo and Katie Furtick, "Thinking about Foreclosures and the Faux-covery," Reason.org, October 24, 2012. Copyright © 2012 by The Reason Foundation. All rights reserved. Reproduced by permission.

of headlines either proclaiming a continued housing recovery or warning that single data points can't be considered in isolation. Housing analysts are notorious for their heterogeneous outlook, so this non-convergence of opinion is to be expected. But can we filter through the headline noise to identify which reports are providing the most robust analysis? Sure, just look for the reports that include a comment or two about a coming foreclosure wave—those are the more robust stories.

The reality is that foreclosures are far from having hit their bottom. They declined after the "robo-signing" scandal in late 2010, which revealed that banks were processing foreclosures too quickly. But this slowdown was the result of procedural changes, not resurgent market strength. A recent Barclay's forecast estimates foreclosures will be rapidly picking up steam going into 2013 and peaking in 2014 before they actually start to dissipate towards the end of 2014 and beyond. We have replicated their forecast to show a few key events that impacted the numbers, below.

The new Massachusetts law, similar to legislation passed in states like Nevada and California and drafted in others, distorts market signals in both housing supply and demand, and less obviously in financial lending.

Putting Downward Pressure on Housing Prices

One of the main reasons that we have been bearish on housing while many others have been declaring a recovery is in motion is that this new wave of foreclosures is certain to put downward pressure on housing prices. The pressure will be highly localized to areas with more heavily concentrated delinquencies—such as South Jersey, South Florida, Mississippi, and Nevada—meaning some areas will be less affected and see price recoveries in the near-term. The nation as a whole, on the other hand, will have to contend with rising foreclosures and the ripple effect that results—unless of course there is some new intervention in the markets to slow down foreclosures again.

Consider, for example, a little talked-about Massachusetts law that will go into effect November 1, 2012 which gives judges in the Bay State the power to determine whether a bank can foreclose on a distressed home, or if it will be forced to modify the homeowner's mortgage to avoid foreclosure. As we wrote at Reason.com last week:

> Signed on August 3 by Gov. Deval Patrick, the "Act Preventing Unlawful and Unnecessary Foreclosures" creates a series of new hoops for banks and other mortgage creditors to jump through in order to foreclose on borrowers who aren't making their payments.
>
> Under the new law, lenders will have to demonstrate to a Massachusetts court that they made "a good faith effort" to work with delinquent borrowers, and that they took "reasonable steps" to avoid foreclosing. Such "steps" would include considering whether the borrower could make a lower "affordable monthly payment" relative to their current delinquent loan.
>
> These terms are ridiculously arbitrary: "reasonable steps" and "affordability" will be defined very differently by a bank trying to get its shareholder's money back, versus a homeowner desperately clinging to a roof over his head. Furthermore, they will be interpreted differently by different judges. . . .

Empowering Judges Less Qualified to Determine Value

The law also requires lenders to prove that they will reap more revenue from foreclosing on the home and selling it in a distressed sale than from modifying the mortgage. At first glance, this provision seems redundant. Presumably a bank would modify a mortgage if they thought they would take fewer losses relative to a foreclosure, even without the government telling them to do so. But the point of the law isn't to encourage banks to figure out how to profit most from delinquent homeowners, it is to empower judges to tell banks that their estimates on value are wrong.

And though judges will soon have that power, they will be far less qualified to determine value than the banks. For instance, implicit in any assessment of whether a foreclosure will be more valuable than a mortgage modification is an estimate of how much selling the home as a bank-owned property would generate. Banks then compare that to the value of a mortgage modification. Not only will a bank and the court likely have different estimations, but from bank to bank there is rarely a concurrence of opinion on housing market futures. This is just the tip of the iceberg in terms of complicating factors for judges and regulators getting into the mortgage value assessment game.

The new Massachusetts law, similar to legislation passed in states like Nevada and California and drafted in others, distorts market signals in both housing supply and demand, and less obviously in financial lending. If a bank is in fact making erroneous estimates on the value of foreclosures, and taking more losses than it needs to rather than modifying mortgages, then judicial intervention will keep the bank in business that should (and prior to this law, would) be allowed to fail. This hurts future financial institutions that would out-compete the bad banks of today, and means poorer quality service for the local areas those banks serve.

More to this newsletter's particular point, this intervention in the foreclosure system slows down the process unnecessarily. Rather than bringing a housing recovery to the near-term, slowing down foreclosures delays the inevitable and pushes any real recovery further off into the future. As long as there is a steady stream of foreclosures in the system, there will be downward pressure on housing prices, and that does not characterize a recovery (at least how I would define one). Whether housing price and sales data over the next week are "positive" or "negative," what really matters is what is going on with the supply of housing and the rate of foreclosures.

10

Repealing the Mortgage Interest Deduction? Hold the Applause!

John C. Weicher

John C. Weicher is director of the Center for Housing and Financial Markets at the Hudson Institute, a conservative Washington, DC, think tank. Weicher was assistant secretary for housing and federal housing commissioner at the US Department of Housing and Urban Development from 2001 to 2005.

The federal government should not repeal the mortgage interest deduction. To do so discourages homeownership and creates a tax-code bias that favors renting. Homeowners are both landlord and tenant—renting to themselves. If the government repeals the mortgage interest deduction, the tax burden becomes greater for homeowners than landlords, thus making homeownership less appealing, particularly for young families. Moreover, claims that only the wealthy benefit from the deduction are flawed. In fact, hardworking middle-class families are the true beneficiaries. In the end, repealing the mortgage interest deduction will discourage families from the eventual gains of homeownership.

President Obama's bipartisan National Commission on Fiscal Responsibility and Reform (commonly referred to as the "Deficit Commission") has called for terminating the mortgage interest deduction for homeowners, and a bipartisan

John C. Weicher, "Repealing the Mortgage Interest Deduction? Hold the Applause!" Hudson Institute, Inc., April 4, 2011. Copyright © 2011 by Hudson Institute, Inc. All rights reserved. Reproduced by permission.

"Gang of Six" senators, four of them members of the Deficit Commission, is now developing a budget plan that is likely to include that recommendation. The deduction is the second largest "tax expenditure" in the entire federal budget; repealing it would bring the federal government more than $100 billion annually. To a Commission trying to cut the deficit by almost $4 trillion over the next decade, it must have looked like a sitting duck.

Although this Commission proposal has been applauded by commentators across the political spectrum, it is bad economic policy.

Part of the rationale for the Commission's recommendation is its desire to have a tax system that is as economically neutral as possible, a tax system that doesn't push people to do something just for the tax advantage. This is a laudable objective and one that nearly every economist favors. Terminating the mortgage interest deduction, however, doesn't help achieve that goal. Instead, it would create a new bias in the tax code, favoring renting rather than owning your own home.

The new Massachusetts law, similar to legislation passed in states like Nevada and California and drafted in others, distorts market signals in both housing supply and demand, and less obviously in financial lending.

Your house is an asset, an investment, as well as a place to live. A homeowner is both an investor and a consumer, both a landlord and a tenant—someone who owns a house and is renting it to himself or herself. Like any other business person, a landlord can deduct business expenses. For rental housing, these include interest on the mortgage, property taxes, maintenance expenditures, and depreciation on the property. At the same time, the landlord has to pay tax on the rent he or she receives, after deducting these business expenses. A homeowner/investor has the same business expenses, but can't deduct all of them. The homeowner can deduct mortgage interest and property taxes, but not maintenance or depreciation. The homeowner also doesn't have to pay taxes on the rental value of the home.

So homeowners have a tax advantage over landlords because owners don't pay taxes on the rental value of their home; and landlords have tax advantages over homeowners because they can deduct maintenance and depreciation, and homeowners can't. But homeowners and landlords are treated equally with respect to mortgage interest and property taxes. Both can deduct these expenses. The recommendation of the Commission takes away the deduction for homeowners, but leaves it in place for landlords.

The President's budget for 2012 proposes to take a small but significant step in the same direction. The value of the deduction would be reduced for families with incomes above $250,000. These are the same taxpayers for whom Mr. Obama wanted to raise taxes back in December—"the rich."

But the deduction isn't a particular benefit for rich people. Taxpayers with incomes above $200,000 are about 5% of all households who pay income taxes—"the richest 5%." They pay over half of all income taxes. But they only account for about 20% of all mortgage interest reported on tax returns, according to the IRS. That is much less than their share of other major deductions; they account for more than half of state and local income taxes, and almost half of charitable contributions.

Most of the benefit of the mortgage interest deduction goes to households who are not "rich," households with incomes between $75,000 and $200,000. These are middle-class families, reasonably well off, but working, and working hard.

Terminating the mortgage interest deduction has other consequences. Homeownership has traditionally been an indicator of middle-class status and a path to financial security. For young families, their first two assets typically are a checking account and a car. Their next two are a home and a 401(k). Those are likely to be their most important assets over the rest of their working lives—particularly their home. For most middle-class families, the equity that they build up in their home is more important than all their financial assets combined. That's also true for lower-income families. Not all of them are homeowners, but about half are, and for them their home is by far their most important asset. Financial assets, such as stocks, bonds, or mutual funds, are concentrated among the wealthiest part of the population. Homeownership and home equity are much more important for the middle class than they are for the rich.

The sooner young families can afford to buy a home, the more likely they are to enjoy an increase in the value of their home, and the greater that increase is likely to be. The mortgage interest deduction makes it easier for them to buy that home, unless they have been lucky enough to enjoy a comfortable inheritance. Most people haven't; they have to work for a living, and work to pay a mortgage as well as their other expenses.

Repealing the mortgage interest deduction will make it harder for young families to become homeowners. Repealing the capital gains exclusion, another Commission recommendation, will make it harder for older families, when they want to move to a retirement home or move to be near their children and grandchildren.

Profiting when you sell your home may seem like a distant dream right now, when foreclosures are rampant and the homeownership rate is declining. Most of the time, however, families that have bought homes have gained financially when they decided to sell. That is the normal experience.

Surveys show that families want to be homeowners, even in today's economy, and they are right. Homeownership has traditionally been an indicator of middle-class status and a path to financial security, and it still is.

11

Tax Reform That Hits Home

Doyle McManus

Doyle McManus is a Los Angles Times *columnist who reports on national and international issues from Washington, DC. He also regularly appears on the Public Broadcasting Service's* Washington Week.

Repealing the mortgage interest deduction would increase the federal treasury and remove an unfair tax advantage for the wealthy. The mortgage interest deduction does not promote homeownership; it promotes debt. Moreover, only those middle-class Americans who itemize their deductions can take advantage of the deduction. Indeed, the mortgage interest deduction tends to benefit those in upper-income brackets. In fact, to develop a fair way to promote homeownership and help the working poor, the government should create a tax credit on mortgages or a cap on tax deductions. Clearly, repealing the mortgage interest deduction would increase federal revenue that the government could better spend lowering taxes or reducing the deficit.

Would you support a tax reform measure that could help reduce the federal deficit, remove a needless distortion in the economy and make the system fairer?

Me too, which is why I'm taking aim at a sacred cow: the home mortgage interest deduction.

That's right, the mortgage interest deduction that every homeowner, including me, loves.

Doyle McManus, "Tax Reform That Hits Home," *Los Angeles Times*, February 6, 2013. Copyright © 2013 by The Los Angeles Times. All rights reserved. Reproduced by permission.

If you listen to home builders and real estate agents, they'll tell you that the mortgage interest deduction is what makes homeownership possible for millions of Americans.

Yet last year, homeownership in the United States, battered by mortgage foreclosures, sank to 65%, a 17-year low, while next door in Canada, where taxpayers don't get a deduction for mortgage interest, homeownership continues to rise, reaching more than 69% last year, according to Toronto's *Financial Post*.

The reason is that our mortgage interest deduction doesn't directly support homeownership; instead, it supports mortgage indebtedness, which isn't the same thing at all.

If the goal is really to increase homeownership, a better idea might be to offer a tax break aimed more precisely at middle-income families buying starter houses—a tax rebate for interest on the first $200,000 in mortgage debt, for example.

But that's not how the mortgage deduction works. First, it's only useful to people who itemize deductions, which only about 30% of taxpayers do. Second, it helps people with big mortgages more than those with small ones. Third, like all deductions, it helps people with the highest incomes (who get the equivalent of 39.6% of their mortgage interest knocked off their tax bill in the top bracket) more than people with lower incomes (who get 25% or less off if they itemize). Moreover, if someone buys a vacation home, that mortgage interest is deductible too, as long as the total debt is under $1 million.

Policy wonks in both political parties believe that trimming the mortgage interest deduction is a good idea.

But don't take it from me. Take it from the economists at the Mercatus Center, a mostly conservative think tank at Virginia's George Mason University.

"Most taxpayers do not benefit from this deduction at all or receive a very small benefit," they wrote in a report issued last month. "The only taxpayers who do receive a large benefit are those in the upper income brackets. . . . Its primary effect is to encourage Americans who would have already been able to afford a house to take on even more debt.

"Recent empirical research suggests that the mortgage interest deduction increases the size of homes purchased but not the overall rate of homeownership," they wrote.

And it's not just conservatives: Policy wonks in both political parties believe that trimming the mortgage interest deduction is a good idea.

President Obama has proposed limiting the value of tax deductions for upper-income taxpayers to 28%, even if they're paying a higher tax rate. But that idea hasn't caught fire.

Mitt Romney, last year's Republican presidential candidate, proposed eliminating all tax deductions for very-high-income taxpayers and putting a cap on deductions—$17,000, for example—for the rest of us. (He wanted lower tax rates too.)

The mortgage interest deduction subsidizes big houses and bigger mortgages, but that's not a good use of tax dollars.

The co-chairmen of Obama's bipartisan debt commission, Alan Simpson and Erskine Bowles, offered a more homeowner-friendly proposal: a 12% tax credit that would go to all taxpayers, even low-income families, on mortgages up to $500,000. (A credit directly reduces your taxes; a deduction merely reduces the amount of your income that's taxed.)

But wait, you and your real estate agent will say. Won't a change in the mortgage interest deduction knock a hole in home values?

Yes—at least at the high end, where high-bracket taxpayers take on million-dollar mortgages. At the lower end, where modest homes are bought by people of modest means? No effect on prices at all, economists say.

And even at the high end, the Mercatus report found, "it is likely to have little effect."

You can be sure that home builders and Realtors, whose businesses thrive on big houses and high prices, will push back hard against any proposal for change.

"We've been preparing for this debate for a year and a half," Jim Tobin, chief lobbyist at the National Assn. of Home Builders, told me recently. "The housing industry is just coming out of its depression," he argued. "This is not the time to dampen that recovery."

OK; not this month, then. But by the end of the year, the economy, and the housing industry, are likely to be in better shape.

The mortgage interest deduction subsidizes big houses and bigger mortgages, but that's not a good use of tax dollars. Its benefits flow disproportionately to the wealthy and do nothing for the working poor.

The deduction currently costs the Treasury about $100 billion a year. That's money we could use to lower taxes, shrink the deficit or pay for Medicare—a debate Obama and the Republicans will surely have.

There aren't many policy changes that would increase government revenue, remove distortion from the economy and make the distribution of income fairer all at the same time.

Fellow homeowners, let's take this one for the team.

12

What to Do with Fannie and Freddie

Alex J. Pollock

Alex J. Pollock is a fellow at the American Enterprise Institute, a conservative think tank that opposes big government and supports privatization and deregulation.

Congress should reduce the monopolistic influence of mortgage finance giants Fannie Mae and Freddie Mac now that the housing crisis these companies helped create is ending. Fannie and Freddie were central culprits in the recent housing bubble and bust, as both inflated real estate prices, encouraged risky lending practices, and over-leveraged housing finance. When the market collapsed, both companies were taken over by the government to keep them solvent and operating. Thus, the US government now owns and runs them. Although Fannie Mae and Freddie Mac have returned to profitability, they nevertheless remain dependent on government backing. The best solution is to completely privatize these government-sponsored enterprises. However, this solution is unlikely in the current, highly partisan Congress. Thus, a plan that reduces the influence of these companies, short of privatization, will enhance the private mortgage market and promote a healthier, less politicized housing sector.

Alex J. Pollock, "What to Do with Fannie and Freddie," *The Journal of the American Enterprise Institute*, May 31, 2013. Copyright © 2013 by American Enterprise Institute. All rights reserved. Reproduced by permission.

Compared to other countries, Fannie Mae and Freddie Mac[1] were and are unique features of U.S. housing finance. They once made U.S. housing finance, according to their own pre-crisis publicity, "the envy of the world." In those days, Fannie and Freddie were accustomed to being the stars and darlings of both Washington and Wall Street—or more precisely, being a darling of Washington made them a star of Wall Street. Fannie in particular was also a greatly feared bullyboy both in Washington and on Wall Street, and most politicians and bankers were afraid to cross or offend it.

Perhaps drunk with power, hubris, the free use of the U.S. Treasury's credit, and nearly unlimited command of other people's money—domestic and international—Fannie and Freddie became major perpetrators of the housing bubble, running up the leverage of the housing finance sector, inflating house prices, escalating systemic risk, and making boodles of bad loans and investments.

As in a Greek tragedy, their hubris led to humiliation. Both went utterly broke, greatly embarrassing their political cheerleaders and allies, including Senator Chris Dodd and Congressman Barney Frank (the chairmen of the respective congressional banking committees), but their taste for using other people's money did not abate. They lost all the profits they had made for the previous 35 years, plus another $150 billion. These enormous losses were foisted on the innocent public, while the government made sure that their creditors, domestic and foreign, were paid every penny on time. Large additional losses to the public are the deadweight bureaucratic costs of the Dodd-Frank Act, sponsored by the aforementioned former political cheerleaders.

1. Congress chartered the Federal National Mortgage Association (Fannie Mae) and the Federal Home Mortgage Corporation (Freddie Mac) to create a secondary market for residential mortgage loans. Both are considered government-sponsored enterprises (GSEs) because Congress authorized their creation and established their public purpose. Together they are the largest source of housing finance in the United States. They were taken over by the federal government to avert their collapse in September 2008 but have since returned to profitability.

Now the housing crisis that Fannie and Freddie made so much worse has finally ended, and the housing cycle is turning back up, as cycles inevitably do. In the meantime, the U.S. housing finance sector has become a largely nationalized and socialized "government housing complex." As the central part of that complex, Fannie and Freddie—now owned by, run by, and simply part of the government—have attained even greater monopoly power and an even more dominant market share than they had before the crisis—an ironic outcome! They have returned to reporting large profits, though they are still completely wards of the U.S. Treasury.

What should be done with Fannie and Freddie is the biggest question surrounding the $10 trillion, post-crisis American housing finance sector, one of the biggest credit markets in the world.

Fannie and Freddie's current large profits are completely dependent on and buttressed by:

a. Being guaranteed by the U.S. Treasury, that is, by the ordinary American taxpayer.

b. Being able to run with zero capital and infinite leverage.

c. Being granted generous and indefensible regulatory loopholes by Dodd-Frank's unfettered bureaucracy, the Consumer Financial Protection Bureau (CFPB). The CFPB is imposing onerous and expensive "ability to pay" regulations on all private housing finance actors, but gives Fannie and Freddie a free pass, thus reinforcing the flow of business into the government.

d. Having the Federal Reserve buy huge amounts—$1 trillion and counting—of Fannie and Freddie's mortgage-backed securities, but of course no private ones, at yields and spreads only a central bank could love. The Fed's mortgage-buying campaign subsidizes and promotes the monopoly powers of Fannie and Freddie.

Having arrived where we are now, what should happen next? What should be done with Fannie and Freddie is the biggest question surrounding the $10 trillion, post-crisis American housing finance sector, one of the biggest credit markets in the world.

Virtually *everybody* agrees that the United States should not return to the flawed—indeed, disastrous—old "government-sponsored enterprise" model of Fannie and Freddie before the crisis, with its warped incentives, runaway leverage, and combination of socialized risk, private profit, and immense political clout. *Nobody* I know of is proposing this.

Congress should enact a medium-term program to move toward a more private, less government-dominated mortgage sector.

But there the consensus ends and the sharp conceptual and ideological divisions begin. Ideally, in my view, Fannie and Freddie's current status, which no one wants, should be brought to an end with a five-year transition. What they do that is actually a mortgage business should be truly privatized (not a fake GSE "privatization" as was done with Fannie in 1968), while their government subsidy program should become explicitly a government subsidy program and be merged into the operations of the Department of Housing, Federal Housing Administration, and Ginnie Mae. Fannie and Freddie would thus cease to exist as GSEs. The U.S. mortgage finance sector would move to being about 80 percent private and 20 percent government, instead of its current heavily nationalized status.

This straightforward program is not likely to be enacted in the current political configuration. Neither are any of the other numerous proposals. But should political stalemate al-

low Fannie and Freddie to continue their status quo indefi-
nitely? If that happens, then, as wards of the government, buttressed by the Treasury, the CFPB, and the Fed, the two will
continue for years to build their monopoly power, probably
leading us in time into a new out-of-control cycle of exces-
sively leveraged and politicized housing finance.

Instead, Congress should enact a medium-term program
to move toward a more private, less government-dominated
mortgage sector, without making final decisions about Fannie
and Freddie's ultimate fate. Such a program could include the
following intermediate steps:

1. Reduce all of Fannie and Freddie's conforming loan limits by 10 percent a year for 7 years, a cumulative reduction of about 50 percent.

2. Continually reduce Fannie and Freddie's mortgage and
   investment portfolios.

3. Change Fannie and Freddie's charters from perpetual to
   limited life charters, with reauthorization required in
   2020.

4. Put more private capital in front of the mortgage credit
   risk of the government. Require credit enhancement of
   Fannie and Freddie's credit risks, by private mortgage
   insurance coverage down to a 70 percent loan-to-value
   ratio (LTV), or equivalent other private credit enhancement. In particular, encourage credit risk retention that
   is junior to Fannie and Freddie's guarantees, by high
   quality mortgage originators, especially by banks and
   savings banks.

5. Create a formal, legally binding definition of the meaning of Prime Mortgage Loan, which further stipulates
   that any mortgage loan which is not prime is nonprime.
   The definition of prime should include a countercyclical LTV/down payment requirement based on the

house price behavior in the relevant market, so that soaring house prices automatically trigger lower LTVs and higher down payments in order to qualify as prime. The extent of taking on nonprime credit risk by Fannie and Freddie should be tightly monitored and limited.

6. Increase the role of local mortgage lenders by authorizing the Federal Home Loan Banks to securitize Prime Mortgage Loans that are all credit enhanced by their member banks and savings banks.

7. Entirely close the giant loopholes created by the CFPB for Fannie and Freddie (and for the FHA). If the CFPB has defined valuable consumer protections in its regulations, such protections should apply to all mortgages, without exception.

8. Stop the Federal Reserve from buying any more Fannie and Freddie mortgage-backed securities, so the MBS market can clear rather than being heavily manipulated by the monetization of mortgages. The housing cycle is definitely rising once again; there is no excuse for the Fed to continue subsidizing the market dominance of Fannie and Freddie.

With such an intermediate program, the private mortgage market could gain market share, while the share of the nationalized Fannie and Freddie would be reduced. We do not have to know in advance exactly how large this healthy shift would ultimately be. We can start moving seriously in what virtually everybody agrees is the right direction.

Organizations to Contact

The editors have compiled the following list of organizations concerned with the issues debated in this book. The descriptions are derived from materials provided by the organizations. All have publications or information available for interested readers. The list was compiled on the date of publication of the present volume; the information provided here may change. Be aware that many organizations take several weeks or longer to respond to inquiries, so allow as much time as possible.

The American Enterprise Institute (AEI)
1150 Seventeenth St. NW, Washington, DC   20036
(202) 862-5800 • fax: (202) 862-7177
e-mail: info@aei.org
website: www.aei.org

The American Enterprise Institute (AEI) is a conservative, libertarian public policy research organization that explores economics, trade, social welfare, government spending and policy, domestic politics, defense, and foreign policy. The Institute publishes books, articles, reports, and its policy magazine, *American Enterprise*. Articles and reports on the housing crisis and housing finance reform are available on its website.

Cato Institute
1000 Massachusetts Ave. NW, Washington, DC   20001-5403
(202) 842-0200 • fax: (202) 842-3490
e-mail: cato@cato.org
website: www.cato.org

Cato Institute is a libertarian public policy research organization that advocates limited government. It publishes a variety of literature concerning the housing crisis and homeownership in its quarterlies *Cato Journal* and *Regulation* and its Policy Analysis series, including the article "Questioning Homeownership as a Policy Goal."

Center for American Progress (CAP)

1333 H St. NW, Washington, DC   20005
(202) 682-1611
website: www.americanprogress.org

The Center for American Progress (CAP) is a progressive public policy research organization whose experts study a variety
of issues, including housing. Many articles and reports on the
housing crisis and homeownership can be found on its housing link, including the reports "Cash for Homes: Policy Impli-
cations of an Investor-Led Housing Recovery" and "Making
the Mortgage Market Work for America's Families."

Consumer Federation of America (CFA)

1620 I St. NW, Suite 200, Washington, DC   20006
(202) 387-6121
e-mail: cfa@consumerfed.org
website: www.consumerfed.org

Consumer Federation of America (CFA) is an association of
nonprofit consumer organizations whose goal is to advance
consumer interests through research, advocacy, and education.
On the CFA website's Housing link, the Federation publishes
press releases, studies, and testimony by its experts on the
Community Reinvestment Act, government-sponsored enterprises, homeownership, and housing finance policy.

Federal Home Loan Mortgage Corporation (Freddie Mac)

8200 Jones Branch Dr., McLean, VA   22102
(703) 903-2000
website: www.freddiemac.com

The Federal Home Loan Mortgage Corporation (Freddie Mac)
is a stockholder-owned company chartered by the federal government to help provide liquidity, stability, and affordability
to the US housing market. It does this by connecting the residential mortgage market to Wall Street and the investment
community through its mortgage purchase, credit guarantee,

and investment activities. The Freddie Mac website includes many resources and provides links to many services that are of interest to homebuyers.

Federal National Mortgage Association (Fannie Mae)
3900 Wisconsin Ave. NW, Washington, DC   20016-2892
(202) 752-7000
website: www.fanniemae.com

The Federal National Mortgage Association (Fannie Mae) was established by the US government in 1938 to facilitate the flow of mortgage funds to communities throughout the country. A shareholder-owned company with a federal charter, Fannie Mae operates in America's secondary mortgage market to ensure that mortgage bankers and other lenders have access to funds to lend to home buyers. On its website Fannie Mae publishes articles on its efforts to support the housing recovery and provides resources to help homeowners avoid foreclosure. The organization also publishes on its website reports on the housing outlook; the latest national housing survey; recent issues of its economic and strategic research monthly, *Housing Insights*; and consumer research articles, including "Renters Are Satisfied, but Continuing to Reach for Homeownership" and "What Motivates Underwater Borrowers to Refinance?"

Joint Center for Housing Studies of Harvard University
1033 Massachusetts Ave., Fifth Floor, Cambridge, MA   02138
(617) 495-7908 • fax: (617) 496-9957
e-mail: jchs@harvard.edu
website: www.jchs.harvard.edu

The Joint Center for Housing Studies of Harvard University analyzes relationships between housing markets and economic, demographic, and social trends in order to provide leaders in government, business, and the nonprofit sector with the knowledge needed to develop effective housing policies and strategies. A list of recent publications located on the Joint Center's website includes the report "The State of the Nation's

Housing 2013," as well as information on the benefits of homeownership, the home mortgage foreclosure crisis, and the housing finance industry.

Mercatus Center, George Mason University

George Mason University, 3351 Fairfax Dr., 4th Floor
Arlington, VA 22201
(703) 993-4930 • fax: (703) 993-4935
website: http://mercatus.org

The Mercatus Center develops and advances market-based solutions to public policy issues, including housing. On its website, on its Financial Markets/Housing & Real Estate link, the Center publishes articles, reports, expert testimony, and commentary on the housing crisis, including "You Don't Need Uncle Sam to Purchase a House" and the compendium *House of Cards: Reforming America's Housing Finance System.*

National Fair Housing Alliance (NFHA)

1101 Vermont Ave. NW, Suite 710, Washington, DC 20005
(202) 898-1661 • fax: (202) 371-9744
e-mail: nfha@nationalfairhousing.org
website: www.nationalfairhousing.org

The National Fair Housing Alliance (NFHA) is a consortium of private, nonprofit fair housing organizations and state and local civil rights agencies with a common interest in combating housing discrimination. It works to ensure equal housing opportunity through leadership, education, advocacy, and enforcement. The Alliance website includes a resource page with a wide range of information relating to housing discrimination before and after the mortgage crisis, including the report "The Banks Are Back—Our Neighborhoods Are Not: Discrimination in the Maintenance and Marketing of REO Properties."

National Housing Conference/Center for Housing Policy

1900 M St. NW, Suite 200, Washington, DC 20036
(202) 466-2121 • fax: (202) 466-2122
website: www.nhc.org

The National Housing Conference/Center for Housing Policy is a nonprofit organization that promotes policies, programs, and legislation to provide affordable and suitable housing for American families. It researches the affordable housing challenges of working-class families and works to create awareness of the need for decent, affordable housing. On its website visitors can find articles, reports, and other publications by using its search engine, perusing its publications, or visiting ancillary organization links such as Foreclosure-Response.org. Reports include "Losing Ground: The Struggle of Moderate-Income Households to Afford the Rising Costs of Housing and Transportation."

National Housing Institute (NHI)

60 S. Fullerton Ave., Suite 202, Montclair, NJ   07042
(973) 509-1600
website: www.nhi.org

The National Housing Institute (NHI) is a nonprofit organization concerned with social and economic equality, health, the environment, education, and sustainability. NHI promotes policies for decent, affordable housing and strong communities. The NHI website search engine provides access to resources related to homeownership, housing, and the mortgage crisis.

US Department of Housing and Urban Development (HUD)

451 7th St. SW, Washington, DC   20410
(202) 708-1112
website: www.hud.gov

The US Department of Housing and Urban Development (HUD) promotes cooperation among federal agencies on housing issues. On its Homeowner Help page on its website, HUD provides links to state and local resources for those who need help with their mortgage, tips on how to avoid foreclosure, and information on the mortgage servicing settlement. Materials on issues concerning housing and homeownership are accessible in its online library.

Bibliography

Books

Edmund Andrew   *Busted: Life Inside the Great Mortgage Meltdown*. New York: W.W. Norton, 2009.

Joseph Fried   *Who Really Drove the Economy into the Ditch?* New York: Algora, 2012.

Laura Gottesdiener   *A Dream Foreclosed: Black America and the Fight for a Place to Call Home*. Westfield, NJ: Zuccotti Park, 2013.

Louis Hyman   *Borrow: The American Way of Debt*. New York: Vintage Books, 2012.

Dan Immergluck   *Foreclosed: High-Risk Lending, Deregulation, and the Undermining of America's Mortgage Market*. Ithaca, NY: Cornell University Press, 2011.

Alyssa Katz   *Our Lot: How Real Estate Came to Own Us*. London/New York: Bloomsbury, 2009.

Peter D. McClelland and Peter H. Tobin   *American Dream Dying: The Changing Economic Lot of the Least Advantaged*. Lanham, MD: Rowman & Littlefield, 2010.

Gretchen Morgenson and Joshua Rosner   *Reckless Endangerment: How Outsized Ambition, Greed, and Corruption Led to Economic Armageddon*. New York: Times Books, 2011.

Neel Kashkari   "Saving Homes Requires Work," *Washington Post*, April 29, 2012.

Barbara Kiviat   "The Case Against Homeownership," *Time*, September 11, 2010.

Arnold Kling   "Freddie Mac and Fannie Mae: An Exit Strategy for the Taxpayer," Cato Institute, September 8, 2008. www.cato.org.

Charles Lane   "It's Time to Fix Fannie Mae and Freddie Mac," *Washington Post*, January 7, 2013.

Mark Lieberman   "Housing Recovery? Hold the Champagne," *DSNews*, May 24, 2013. www.dsnews.com.

Steven Malanga   "Obsessive Housing Disorder," *City*, Spring 2009.

Barbara Mantel   "Future of Homeownership," *CQ Researcher*, December 14, 2012.

Vicki Needham   "Fannie, Freddie Profits Could Sap Will in Congress to Reform Mortgage Giants," *The Hill*, May 12, 2013.

Alexei Painter   "Home Mortgage Interest Deduction Vulnerable," *San Francisco Chronicle*, October 26, 2012.

Edward J. Pinto   "Five Myths About the Federal Housing Administration," *Roll Call*, May 3, 2013.

Jim Powell "Housing Crisis? Look to Canada for Answers," *AOL News*, September 3, 2010. www.aol.com.

Cathy Reisenwitz "How Obama's Plan to Encourage Homeownership Will Hurt the Poor the Most," *Reason*, April 3, 2013.

David Reiss "Fannie Mae, Freddie Mac, and the Future of Federal Housing Finance Policy: A Study of Regulatory Privilege," *Policy Analysis*, April 18, 2011.

Jacob S. Rugh and Douglas S. Massey "Racial Segregation and the American Foreclosure Crisis," *American Sociological Review*, October 2010.

Anthony Sanders "Leaving Fannie Mae, Freddie Mac as Is Risks Another Housing Bubble," *U.S. News & World Report*, May 15, 2012.

Joseph E. Stiglitz and Mark Zandi "The One Housing Solution Left: Mass Mortgage Refinancing," *New York Times*, August 12, 2012.

Nick Timiraos "Home Sales Power Optimism," *Wall Street Journal*, May 28, 2013.

Washington Times "Housing Market Follies," September 21, 2011.

Index

H

I

J

Jefferson, Thomas, 7
Johnson, James, 12

L

Lending reform
   cutting back lending, 55–56
   economic growth and, 46–47
   middle-class homeownership
    and, 41–42
   minority homeownership,
    53–57
   mortgage credit and, 40–47
   overview, 40–41, 53
   as protection, 54–55
   renters vs. buyers, 45–46
   risk retention rule, 43–44
Loans
   high-risk, low-cost loans, 51
   interest-only loans, 49
   negative amortization loans,
    49
   no-doc loans, 49
   no down payment loans, 12
   no-interest loans, 54
   real estate loans, 8
   risky loans, 36–37
   safe harbor and loans, 50
   subprime loans, 34, 37
   timeshare loans, 50
   See also Federal Home Loan
    Mortgage Corporation;
    Mortgages; Racist lending
Loan-to-value ratio (LTV), 82–83
Long-term government bonds, 27
Long-term mortgages, 9–10
Los Angeles Times (newspaper), 14
Lovenheim, Michael F., 46–47
Low-income urban residents, 11
Low-risk mortgages, 9

M

Malanga, Steven, 8–9, 13
Manhattan Institute, 8–9
McManus, Doyle, 74–77
Mercatus Center, 75, 77
Middle-class households
   homeownership and, 41–42
   housing subsidies and, 29
   lending to, 12
   mortgage interest deduction,
    72–73
Minority homeownership
   discrimination against, 10, 11,
    36
   lending reform threatens,
    53–57
Mortgage credit, 40–47, 67, 82
Mortgage debt, 20, 28, 75
Mortgage finance, 45, 81
Mortgage holder, 20
Mortgage interest deduction
   benefit of, 72–73
   disadvantages of, 27–29,
    76–77
   should be repealed, 74–77
   should not be repealed, 70–73
Mortgages
   adjustable rate mortgages, 12
   American Dream and, 52
   at-risk mortgages, 9, 18
   distressed mortgages, 22
   down payments for, 43
   falling behind on payments,
    62
   first-lien mortgage, 55
   long-term mortgages, 9–10
   low-income mortgages, 13–14,
    76
   low-risk mortgages, 9
   modifications to, 68
   prime mortgages, 64
   for a public purpose, 20

Z